Asteroid Impact!
Revelation Foretells Our End

By Walter Parks

Copyright 2013
UnKnownTruths
Publishing Company

UnKnownTruths
Publishing Company
8815 Conroy Windermere Rd. Ste 190
Orlando, FL 32835
UnknownTruths.com
info@UnknownTruths.com

1

Contents

Introduction

And the stars of heaven fell unto the Earth….Revelation 6:13

An asteroid will destroy mankind just as one destroyed the dinosaurs.

The Book of Revelation in the Bible reveals to us that this is our destiny.

And I beheld when he had opened the sixth seal, and, lo, there was a great Earthquake; and the sun became black as sackcloth of hair, and the moon became as blood; Revelation 6:12

Matthew supports this:

Immediately after the tribulation of those days shall the sun be darkened, and the moon shall not give her light, and the stars shall fall from heaven, and the powers of the heavens shall be shaken: Matthew 29.

Joel also supports this:

I will show wonders in the heavens and on the Earth, blood and fire and billows of smoke. The sun will be turned to darkness and the moon to blood before the coming of the great and dreadful day of the Lord. Joel 2:30-31

Isaiah also supports this:

And they shall go into the holes of the rocks, and into the caves of the Earth, for fear of the Lord, and for the glory of his majesty, when he ariseth to shake terribly the Earth. Isaiah 2:19

And in Ezekiel we also read about the darkness of the sun, moon, and stars.

The basic message of all of this is that in the end times we will all be destroyed by an asteroid impacting Earth.

To understand and assess the truth of all of this, we need to review the purpose of Revelation, who wrote it, and why and how it was written.

And we need to better understand the seals that were broken to reveal our future.

How accurate are these Biblical predictions?

What are the scientific facts upon which the predictions are based?

And from a scientific standpoint, how likely is it that an asteroid will destroy us?

Let's review all of this.

We will see that Revelation's foretelling will almost surely come to pass.

Chapter 1
Book of Revelation

And there was war in heaven: Michael and his angels fought against the dragon; and the dragon fought and his angels,

And prevailed not; neither was their place found any more in heaven. **Revelation 12:7-8**

The Book of Revelation tells us that we will be destroyed by an asteroid.

We will see that other parts of the Bible and many ancient documents support this assertion.

We will show the scientific proof that the "dragon" which Michael fought was remnants from an asteroid that was created by the Vela Supernova.

We will describe the date of the event, how it happened and what it did to planet Earth.

The Book of Revelation has been described as a summation of all the prophetic writings of the Bible. It was written to give the revelations of the fate of the Church and the world.

The Book of Revelation was inspired and parts of it were written by "John", mostly while in exile on the Island of Pathos.

Before we proceed let's try to describe just who John really was, who helped him write Revelation and where the writers got their information.

Who Wrote Revelation

John "assembled" the Book of Revelation. We can tell from his writings that he was a devout Jew/Christian. We also know from various literatures that he was a "mystic" that was exiled on the island of Patmos, off the coast of present-day Greece.

Patmos is a Greek island in the Dodecanese group, located about 40 miles west of the western coast of Turkey.

It is said that it was here while exiled that John received the revelation that he wrote about in the New Testament book of Revelation (Revelation 1:9).

Tradition maintains that the Roman authorities exiled him to Patmos during the reign of the Roman Emperor Domitian (A.D. 81–96). This tradition is credible because banishment was a common punishment used during the Imperial period for a number of offenses. Among such offenses was prophecy which was perceived as a threat to Roman political power and order.

John was eventually released and returned to Ephesus which is located about 60 miles to the northeast of Patmos.

The text of Revelation states that the author is called John and that he lives on the Greek island of Patmos.

Traditionally, the John who is the author of Revelation is considered to be John the Apostle, author of the Gospel of John, the first, second, and third epistles of John, as well as Revelation.

However, in the case of Revelation, many modern scholars agree that it was written by a separate, otherwise unknown author to whom they have given the name John of Patmos, who was believed to be an early Church official.

Others believe that Revelation was written by Cerinthus who was a Gnostic teacher in the last days of John the Apostle. Cerinthus was very controversial. He taught that God did not create the world and he denied the divinity of Jesus.

All of these believers are likely wrong to believe that Revelation was written by a single author.

It is likely that a portion of Revelation was written by the Apostle John with more than 90% of Revelation being written by others, including the unknown John of Pathos. Several others, probably long after the Gospel of John was written (about 95 AD) continued to write and rewrite Revelation. Some of these others may also have also been called John.

It should also be noted that there was a tradition for a disciple to attribute his own writing to his teacher.

There have been a number of analyses to try to see who wrote Revelation. One such analysis noted that "Dragon" never appears in the four Gospels, never in Jesus teachings, but appears numerous times in the Revelation. John never heard the word "dragon" from Jesus' teachings. **But we will see later where the author got "dragon".**

John never mentioned Hades or hell in his Gospel. Hell is an important concept in the Revelation.

This is evidence that John alone did not write all of Revelation.

Among the documents that John studied in order to write Revelation was a very ancient one written by the scribe that documented the experiences of people hiding in a cave during the events that appear to be destroying the Earth; we'll discuss this in great detail later.

I like to think that John the Apostle was the principle initiator of the "assembly" that came to be Revelation. He had ample time to accumulate copies of the ancient writings from which Revelation was constructed.

At the Emperor's death in 97 AD John returned to Ephesus where he lived to a ripe old age.

Why Was Revelation Written

John had experienced a catastrophe. He wrote his book not long after 60,000 Roman soldiers had stormed Jerusalem in 70 A.D., burned down its great temple and left the city in ruins after putting down an armed Jewish revolt.

For some of the earliest Jewish followers of Jesus, the destruction of Jerusalem was incomprehensible. They had expected Jesus to return "with power" and conquer Rome before inaugurating a new age. But Rome had conquered Jesus' homeland instead.

One of John's purposes in writing Revelation was to encourage the followers of Jesus at a time when their world seemed doomed.

Revelation was an anti-Roman document and a piece of war propaganda wrapped in one. The message: God would return and destroy the Romans who had destroyed Jerusalem.

John was deeply angry and grieved by what Rome had done in this Jewish war and by the great damage that they had done to his people.

But John was just one of many writers who voiced concerns and complaints during this traumatic time.

Early church leaders suppressed a very large number of books that claimed to be revelations from apostles such as Peter and James. Many of these books continued to be read and treasured by Christians throughout the Roman Empire.

But only Revelation made it into the Bible.

Bishop Athanasius Made Revelation Part of the Bible

The decision to include Revelation was made primarily by Bishop Athanasius who championed Revelation about 360 years after the death of Jesus.

Athanasius was so fiery that during his 46 years as bishop he was deposed and exiled five times.

He was primarily responsible for shaping the New Testament while excluding books he labeled as hearsay.

Many church leaders opposed including Revelation in the New Testament. Athanasius's predecessor had said the book was "unintelligible, irrational and false."

Athanasius though saw Revelation as a useful political tool. He transformed it into an attack ad against Christians who questioned him.

By this time Rome was no longer the enemy; Athanasius felt that those who questioned church authority were the real foes of Christianity.

Athanasius interpreted Revelation's cosmic war as a crusade against heretics and reads John's visions as a sharp warning to Christian dissidents.

Even today Revelation still is the most controversial book in the Bible.

Purpose and Messages of Revelation

Perhaps John's purpose for Revelation was too broad and he incorporated too many ancient thoughts and concepts.

John researched an enormous number of ancient writings in his attempt to summarize all of the prophetic writings of the Bible.

His main purpose was to reveal and summarize the prophecies to tell Christians about the return of Jesus and **what the future held for them.**

Piecing together many parts from the ancient literature resulted in a document that carried forward archaic language and analogous symbols from the past. **This is why Revelation is so very difficult to read and understand.**

John did not reveal how he pieced all the ancient information together but rather led the reader to understand that the resurrected Lord came in spirit to him in the year 95-96 A.D. on the Isle of Patmos, where he had been banished for inciting the population about Christianity.

Throughout the book of Revelation John describes angelic messengers bringing messages to him on Patmos.

John describes his finished book of Revelation as a scroll with seven wax seals. As we open it and begin to read, we get this unfolding scenario of events beginning with war and famine and disease and Earthquakes and heavenly signs.

As you continue to read you are introduced to six main characters. One is the false prophet. He's like a dragon, but he speaks like a lamb. He has horns; he is a beast that is non-descript, some sort of horrible creature that appears to stand for the Roman government to the early Christians. **I believe I found this creature and will describe him in a later Chapter.**

Revelation tells us that there will be wars and famines and disease epidemics and heavenly signs that will alert the world to a crisis.

As the book continues we are told of Asteroids hitting the Earth; of water turning to blood and other happenings that sound mythical.

Then Jesus Christ returns as a warrior on a white horse and sets up the kingdom of God.

Revelation is essentially a book about the wrath of God being poured out upon the world and **how life on Earth ends.**

Let's review a bit of it starting with Revelation 8:7.

The first angel sounded, and there followed hail and fire mingled with blood, and they were cast upon the Earth:

12

and the third part of trees was burnt up, and all green grass was burnt up.

And the second angel sounded, and as it were a great mountain burning with fire was cast into the sea: and the third part of the sea became blood;

Remember this **"great mountain burning with fire (that) was cast into the sea".** I describe the scientific proof of just what this was in a later Chapter.

And the third part of the creatures which were in the sea, and had life, died; and the third part of the ships were destroyed.

And the third angel sounded, and there fell a great star from heaven, burning as it were a lamp, and it fell upon the third part of the rivers, and upon the fountains of waters; Revelation 8:7-10

Let's skip to Revelation 9:01.

And the fifth angel sounded, and I saw a star fall from heaven unto the Earth: and to him was given the key of the bottomless pit.

And he opened the bottomless pit; and there arose a smoke out of the pit, as the smoke of a great furnace; and the sun and the air were darkened by reason of the smoke of the pit. Revelation 9:1-2

Let's skip to Revelation 9:18.

By these three was the third part of men killed, by the fire, and by the smoke, and by the brimstone, which issued out of their mouths.

For their power is in their mouth, and in their tails: for their tails were like unto serpents, and had heads, and with them they do hurt. Revelation 9:18-19

Remember the serpents; I explain them scientifically in a later Chapter.

And he said unto me, Thou must prophesy again before many peoples, and nations, and tongues, and kings. Revelation 13:18

Let's skip to Revelation 16:01.

And I heard a great voice out of the temple saying to the seven angels, Go your ways, and pour out the vials of the wrath of God upon the Earth.

And the first went, and poured out his vial upon the Earth; and there fell a noisome and grievous sore upon the men which had the mark of the beast, and upon them which worshipped his image.

And the second angel poured out his vial upon the sea; and it became as the blood of a dead man: and every living soul died in the sea.

And the third angel poured out his vial upon the rivers and fountains of waters; and they became blood. Revelation 16:1-4

Let's skip to Revelation 16:08.

And the fourth angel poured out his vial upon the sun; and power was given unto him to scorch men with fire.

And men were scorched with great heat, and blasphemed the name of God, which hath power over these plagues: and they repented not to give him glory.

And the fifth angel poured out his vial upon the seat of the beast; and his kingdom was full of darkness; and they gnawed their tongues for pain,

And blasphemed the God of heaven because of their pains and their sores, and repented not of their deeds.

And the sixth angel poured out his vial upon the great river Euphrates; and the water thereof was dried up, that the way of the kings of the east might be prepared. Revelation 16:8-12

Remember that the River Euphrates dried up; I explain the scientific basis for this in a later Chapter. Let's skip o Revelation 16:16.

And he gathered them together into a place called in the Hebrew tongue Armageddon.

And the seventh angel poured out his vial into the air; and there came a great voice out of the temple of heaven, from the throne, saying, It is done.

And there were voices, and thunders, and lightnings; and there was a great Earthquake, such as was not since men were upon the Earth, so mighty an Earthquake, and so great.

And the great city was divided into three parts, and the cities of the nations fell: and great Babylon came in remembrance before God, to give unto her the cup of the wine of the fierceness of his wrath.

And every island fled away, and the mountains were not found.

And there fell upon men a great hail out of heaven, every stone about the weight of a talent: and men blasphemed God because of the plague of the hail; for the plague thereof was exceeding great. Revelation 16:16-21

Let's skip to Revelation 20:01.

And I saw an angel come down from heaven, having the key of the bottomless pit and a great chain in his hand.

And he laid hold on the dragon, that old serpent, which is the Devil, and Satan, and bound him a thousand years,

And cast him into the bottomless pit, and shut him up, and set a seal upon him, that he should deceive the nations no more, till the thousand years should be fulfilled: and after that he must be loosed a little season. Revelation 20:1-3

Let's skip to Revelation 20:10.

And the devil that deceived them was cast into the lake of fire and brimstone, where the beast and the false prophet are, and shall be tormented day and night for ever and ever.

And I saw a great white throne, and him that sat on it, from whose face the Earth and the heaven fled away; and there was found no place for them.

And I saw the dead, small and great, stand before God; and the books were opened: and another book was opened, which is the book of life: and the dead were judged out of those things which were written in the books, according to their works.

And the sea gave up the dead which were in it; and death and hell delivered up the dead which were in them: and they were judged every man according to their works.

And death and hell were cast into the lake of fire. This is the second death.

And whosoever was not found written in the book of life was cast into the lake of fire. Revelation 20:10-15

Let's go to Revelation 21:01.

And I saw a new heaven and a new Earth: for the first heaven and the first Earth were passed away; and there was no more sea.

And I John saw the holy city, new Jerusalem, coming down from God out of heaven, prepared as a bride adorned for her husband. Revelation 21:1-2

So we can see that the Book of Revelation is very difficult to read and understand. And we now know from analyses that its difficulty stems from it having been pieced together from several ancient documents that were written earlier to explain the great disaster caused by an asteroid impacting Earth.

It is easier to understand when we see the scientific evidence for the great disaster presented in a later Chapter. But let's first note the other Biblical References to the Disaster.

Chapter 2
Other Biblical References to the Disaster

*And I will shew wonders in the heavens and in the Earth,
....blood, and fire, ...and pillars of smoke. The Earth and the
heavenly bodies will go into convulsions.* **Joel 2:30-31**

This terrible disaster and Earthquakes are also told about in Isaiah 2:19:

And they shall go into the holes of the rocks, and into the caves of the Earth, for fear of the Lord, and for the glory of his majesty, when he ariseth to shake terribly the Earth.

Remember this passage; you will see in a later Chapter that we found an ancient document written long before John wrote Revelation that records the events as written by some people hiding in a cave.

In Ezekiel 32:7-8, we also read about the darkness of the sun, moon, and stars.

In Matthew 24:29, we read of this same thing in the heavens.

Immediately after the tribulation of those days shall the sun be darkened, and the moon shall not give her light, and the stars shall fall from heaven, and the powers of the heavens shall be shaken.

In Luke 21:25-26, we read again of the commotion in heaven:

And there shall be signs in the sun, and in the moon, and in the stars; and upon the Earth distress of nations, with perplexity; the sea and the waves roaring; Men's hearts failing them for fear, and for looking after those things which are coming on the Earth: for the powers of heaven shall be shaken.

You can easily see that this disaster is prophesied, not just by John, but by dozens of writers throughout the Bible.

Now note Revelation 6:15:

And the kings of the Earth, and the great men, and the rich men, and the chief captains, and the mighty men, and every bondman, and every free man, hid themselves in the dens and in the rocks of the mountains.

We found a very ancient document written by witnesses to the disaster that hid in a cave. We give the details of this ancient document in a later Chapter.

Let's first describe the natural, scientific facts upon which parts of Revelation were based.

Chapter 3
The Scientific Basis for Revelation

At the heart of science is an essential balance between two seemingly contradictory attitudes, an openness to new ideas, no matter how bizarre or counterintuitive they may be, and the most ruthless skeptical scrutiny of all ideas, old and new. This is how deep truths are winnowed from deep nonsense. **Carl Sagan**

There is a scientific basis for the War in Heaven and for John's forecasts of the future in Revelation.

Satan was indeed thrown from heaven. Satan was a very large object from the explosion of the Vela Supernova.

The Vela Supernova

A rather large, but otherwise common star in the constellation of Vela, situated about 45 light years away from our solar system, became a supernova and exploded sometimes between 14,300 and 11,000 years ago. This can be approximated by observable debris fields.

The most visible remains of the supernova is the Vela Supernova Remnant as depicted. It is indeed interesting that it actually has the uncanny appearance (when seen in color) of the popular conception of Satan!

**The Vela Supernova Remnant;
Satan's original home in heaven!**

Supernovae occur at the end of the lives of massive stars, when they have exhausted their nuclear fuel. The star begins to collapse into its self and then explodes, releasing as much energy in a few days as is normally emitted in the same time period by the entire galaxy of billions of stars.

The typical remains are the nebulae as depicted. There is usually a pulsar imbedded near the nebula's center. Vela's pulsar is a rapidly spinning neutron star of intense density, but having a very small diameter. It spins about 11 times a second.

Such a supernova is not a rare event in the universe. Several have been observed in a single year. However supernovae are rare in our own Milky Way Galaxy. The last supernova in our galaxy was Cassiopeia, which was first viewable from Earth in 1680 AD. It is 9 to 11 thousand light years from Earth, near the edge of our Milky Way Galaxy, so it actually exploded sometime between 9323 and 11323 years ago.

In ancient Ethiopia, Cassiopeia was believed to be the mother of Andromeda. We now recognize Andromeda as another galaxy and Cassiopeia as the remains of the youngest supernova in our Milky Way Galaxy.

Cassiopeia was the last supernova is our galaxy.

An earlier supernova, first seen in 1054 AD, created the better-known Crab Nebula as depicted. It is about 6 thousand light years from Earth; therefore it exploded almost 7 thousand years ago. Its pulsar spins about 30 times per second.

The Crab Nebula is the remnant of a supernova that occurred in 1054 AD.

The Hubble Space Telescope photographed a more recent supernova, named "Super Nova 1987 A" for the year in which it became visible on Earth. It is 167 thousand light years from Earth, thus it exploded about 167 thousand years ago, with its light finally reaching Earth February 23, 1987.

**The Hubble Space Telescope photographed
Supernova 1987A February 23, 1987.**

Betelgeuse is expected to be the next major star in our galaxy to become a supernova. It is 425 light years away. When it goes, it will be visible all day and cast a light at night.

Betelgeuse makes up the right shoulder of the constellation Orion. It is interesting to note that Orion was a major feature in the religions of many ancient peoples, and is believed by many to be a model for the layout of the pyramids of Gaza in Egypt.

The heavens are full of supernova remnants. But none of them can match the interest of Vela! Vela was the ancient source of Satan and now appears as our poplar face of Satan!

The Vela supernova probably ejected a mass of material about 1.4 times the size of our sun. A chunk of this material, calculated to be a little larger than our Earth, was hurled towards our solar system at an average speed of between 1 percent and 10 percent the speed of light. Calculations suggest that the most likely average speed was 1/62 the speed of light.

This mass of material would have been a glob of glowing hot matter. It would have been pulled into an elongated sphere by its own gravity, combined with the slightly varying velocities of adjacent materials.

Some of the additional expelled materials, slightly farther away from the largest mass would have then been gravitationally attracted to this very large mass. These additional materials would have become a stream of trailing materials that tended to rotate about the center of mass of the largest mass.

After a time, this combined "chunk" of materials would have begun to appear to be the glowing hot, bigheaded serpent described in the ancient literature. It would appear to undulate because of the rotation of parts of the trailing materials.

Kuiper Belt Encounters

This chunk, with its streaming tail of materials, arrived in our solar system about 11,500 years ago. It is important to note that it was "going the wrong way", i.e. it was going in the opposite direction of the planets orbiting our sun. And it was going in an opposing direction to the sub-planets and other objects in the Kuiper Belt of objects out beyond the orbit of Pluto.

It is most likely that the chunk of materials encountered one or more bodies in the Kuiper Belt.

It is believed that there are millions of objects in this belt. Over 600 such objects have been cataloged. Most of the objects are too small to be seen from Earth, but it is estimated that 70,000 or more are at least 60 miles in diameter, and many are known to be 150 miles or more in diameter. One, dubbed KBO, with a diameter of 800 miles, was recently spotted.

Collisions with objects in the Kuiper Belt most likely fractured the main and extended body of the chunk, creating an even longer "tail" of materials. Some of these smaller pieces would have had a tendency to orbit, in a corkscrew like fashion, about the larger mass. These smaller pieces would also further disperse over time and form an ever increasingly longer tail. Such a swarm of objects would come to look more and more like a bigheaded, perhaps multi-headed, serpent with a long undulating tail.

Neptune Encounter

At the time that the chunk entered our solar system, the outermost planet was Neptune. It is believed that Pluto, previously the ninth and farthest out planet, but now relegated to a dwarf planet, was then a moon of Neptune. It has also been speculated that Neptune had earlier captured Pluto from the Kuiper Belt.

An ancient Sumerian tablet suggests that Marduk, the Sumerian name for the chunk which the Hebrews called Satan, may have pulled Pluto from its orbit around Neptune and set it back on its own orbit, which the Sumerians called its own "destiny".

As the chunk continued on its path towards the sun, the gravity from the giant Neptune began to influence it. Neptune is 17.14 times more massive than is Earth.

When it was close enough to Neptune, the two bodies began to exchange great lighting-like electromagnetic discharges, as the bodies tended to equalize their very different charges.

This is when the gravity of the chunk exerted a pull on Neptune's moon Pluto and caused Pluto to be pulled from its orbit around Neptune, and slung into its own orbit around the sun.

Pluto has the most irregular orbit of all the planets and dwarf planets. It is the only dwarf planet that crosses the orbit of another planet, in that it regularly still crosses Neptune's orbit, as it did when it originally rotated around Neptune as its moon. The plane

27

of Pluto's orbit also deviates most from the planes of the other planets. It is 17.148 degrees from Earth's orbit plane.

So there is considerable evidence that Pluto was a moon of Neptune that was slung into its own, irregular orbit by a large body passing close-by. The irregular orbits of Neptune's remaining two moons, Triton and Nereid, also support such a disturbance as would be caused by this passing.

Neptune's mass, more than 13 times the mass of the chunk, plus its very close proximity at the passing, presented a gravitational field that caused Neptune's tides of gravity to break-up the chunk into even more of a swarm of many pieces of greatly varying sizes.

Neptune's gravitational pull at this close approach was very much greater than the pull from the distant sun. This resulted in the chunk's path being altered towards a tendency to orbit Neptune on a highly elliptical orbit.

Uranus Encounter

The chunk, on this altered orbit, approached the orbit of Uranus. Uranus has about 85 percent of the mass, and thus gravitational pull of Neptune; but when the chunk came near Uranus, its attraction was much greater than the more distant Neptune or the distant sun.

Uranus was already pass the possible impact point, but the bodies passed close enough to exchange electromagnetic discharges and Uranus's gravitational pull was sufficient to detach at least 4 pieces from the broken chunk.

This encounter:

1 Provided Uranus with at least 4 of its now 17 moons;

2 Turned Uranus's axis of rotation to 97 degrees 55 minutes (compared to Earth's 23 degrees 27 minutes);

3 Distorted Uranus's magnetic field 59 degrees from its axis of rotation, and 15 percent away from the planet's center (It had also produced a similar off-center field in Neptune.)

4 Again altered the chunk's orbit to an elongated ellipse, now about Uranus.

Saturn Encounter

Saturn's mass is over 6.5 times that of Uranus; so soon after the chunk left the vicinity of Uranus, the primary gravitational attraction came from Saturn.

Saturn mass is 80 times greater than the chunk's. It altered the chunk's path causing a very near pass-by. One of Saturn's moons, Chiron, which was in its orbit far from Saturn, passed extremely close to the chunk, and was pulled out of orbit and sent on its own destiny (orbit) around the sun, similar to the manner in which the chunk had torn Pluto from Neptune and placed it in its own orbit.

Chiron was known in ancient times as Kronus's (Saturn's) son, as described in Sumerian clay tablets. (How did the ancient Sumerians know that tiny Chiron had been Saturn's moon?)

When Chiron was later "discovered" by modern science, it was deemed too small to be called a planet. It is only 1,419 miles in diameter. It is now classified as a dwarf planet as is Pluto.

As the chunk continued to approach Saturn, gravitational tides began to fracture the chunk and parts of it began to disperse. Saturn's great gravity then pulled a piece of the broken up chunk into orbit around it.

It is interesting that this new moon of Saturn's, Phoebe, orbits in a retrograde orbit; i.e. circles in the opposite direction of the other moons. This was probably caused by the fact that the chunk had been going in this "opposite direction".

It is also possible, however, that this piece of the chunk may have been one of the pieces that had been orbiting the chunk when the chunk approached Saturn. It may have been captured by the chunk in one of the chunk's previous encounters as opposed to being an original part of the chunk from Vela.

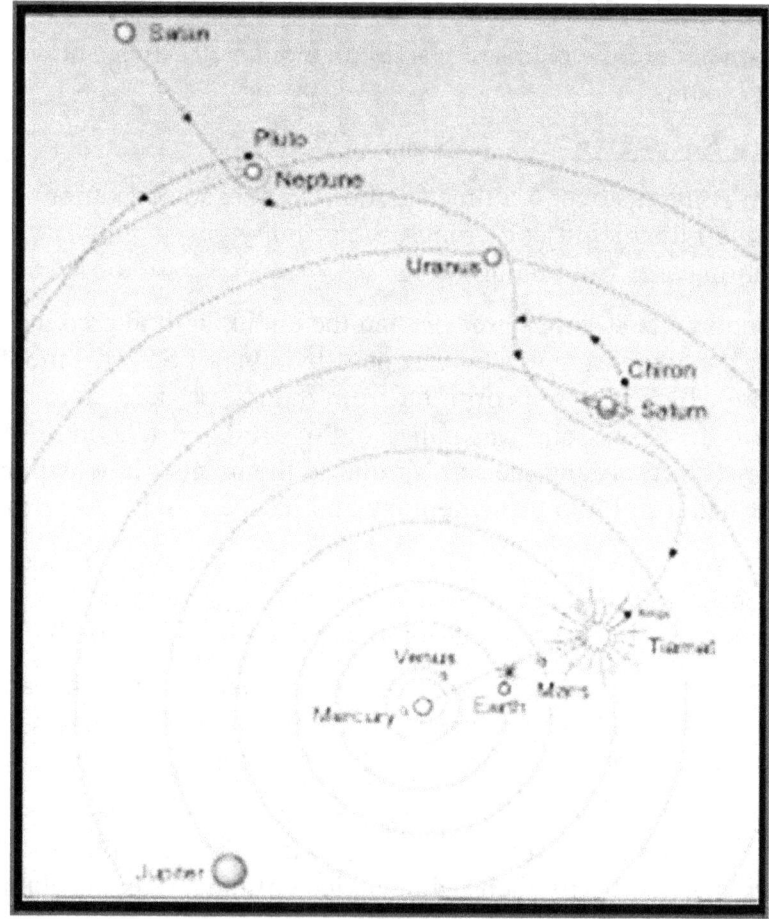

The planets continuously changed the chunk's orbit.

Wrong Way Orbit

The chunk then continued on its elongated orbit about Saturn until it was far enough away from Saturn that the sun's gravitational field became more dominate, and began to pull the chunk's orbit back towards the sun.

At this time the giant planet Jupiter was in its orbit on the other side of the sun so it did not influence the chunk's path.

So the chuck's orbital path had by this time experienced the following transitions:

1 Hurled from the supernova generally towards the solar system;

2 Drawn towards the sun;

3 Drawn towards Neptune and established in an elliptical orbit about Neptune, but before it could complete even half an orbit;

4 Drawn towards Uranus and established in an elongated ellipse about Uranus, but again, before it could complete much of the orbit;

5 Drawn towards the very much larger Saturn, and again, before it could complete much of the orbit;

6 Drawn towards Tiamat as Tiamat's pull became stronger as the chunk left the vicinity of Saturn.

All of this time, the chunk's orbit was "going the wrong way", relative to all the planets. There are several ancient accounts that refer to this wrong way orbit, including the writings of Ovid which is presented later.

Tiamat: The Destroyed Planet

At the time of the chunk's intrusion into the solar system, there was a large planet in the orbit now occupied by the asteroid belt. The ancients knew about it and had named it Tiamat. It had a mass 90 times that of the chunk, so it soon became the most dominate attracting force.

31

Modern science does not know about Tiamat because this planet was destroyed, as described below, before the modern era. Most scientists consider the Sumerian stories of Tiamat to be myths.

But very compelling evidence shows that Tiamat was well known to the ancient world. It was the brightest star in the heavens (after the sun and moon). It was believed to be the mother god, and was widely worshipped in the ancient world.

The planets known by the ancient Sumerians are depicted on a tablet.

The planets know by the Ancient Sumerians are depicted in the upper left.

Larger view of the planets known to the ancients from above tablet.

The Sumerian names for the planets are as follows:

Upper row:

Far left: Tiamat which was destroyed and its fragments are now the asteroid belt.

Second from left: Lahmu which we call Mars.

Third from left: Ki which we call Earth.

Fourth from left: Sin which we call the Moon.

Second row:

Far left: Kishar which we call Jupiter.

Second from left: the Sun.

Third from left: Mommu which we call Mercury.

Fourth from left: Lahamu which we call Venus.

33

Bottom row:

Far left: Anshar which we call Saturn

Second from left: Gaga which we have termed a dwarf planet and call it Chiron.

Third from left: Anu which we call Uranus.

Fourth from left: Ea and sometimes Nudimmud which we call Neptune.

Tiamat Encounter

The combined pulls from Tiamat and the sun turned the chunk from its orbit about Saturn and the sun, and caused it to approach Tiamat. The two bodies exchanged great electromagnetic discharges to equalize their very different electromagnetic charges.

The great mass of Tiamat forced an impact. Debris was hurled all over the where. Some stayed in orbit around the sun and became the asteroid belt. Some experienced various elongated orbits about the sun and added to the number of comets and other materials that orbit and "wander" about the solar system. Some escaped from the solar system.

But most of the debris from the collision had too little velocity to remain in orbit because the angle of impact had countered each body's velocity. This resulting mass began to spiral towards the sun.

One large member of this mass was Tiamat's principle moon, Kingu. As the remains of Tiamat and the chunk spiraled towards the sun, Kingu continued to orbit, in a corkscrew fashion about the combined remaining mass of Tiamat and the chunk.

From Earth, the sky appeared to be filled with heavenly bodies, i.e. pieces from the collision. There were probably many, many thousands; perhaps millions. However, many were too small to be seen from Earth, and many were clumped close enough together such that they would appear as one. All together, the stream of materials appeared as a great undulating, fiery serpent.

Kingu and other objects orbiting the materials from the collision made the "serpent's" motion appear very dynamic.

As this now extended stream of undulating materials spiraled towards the sun, it approached the orbit of Mars.

Mars Encounter

At this time Mars was too far from its orbit crossing point to cause an impact, but the bodies passed close enough to exchange electromagnetic discharges. The passing was also close enough to:

1 Greatly reduce Mars' magnetic field;

2 Fracture Mars' crust;

3 Upset Mars' rotational equilibrium such that it was slowed from its then 8 hour day to slightly more than a 24 hour day;

4 Send Mars into a much more eccentric orbit;

5 Cause Mars to pull 2 very irregularly shaped, jagged, pieces of rock from the stream of Tiamat and chunk debris.

These 2 moons of Mars are the most jagged moons in the known universe.

Earth Encounter

The stream of material, still being orbited by Tiamat's moon, Kingu, continued on its path towards the sun, and Earth.

The stream of material was clearly visible, not only in the night sky, but had become visible in full daylight. Ancient literature state that:

For 10 nights it looked like a man;

For 10 nights it then looked like a golden horned bull;

For 10 nights it then looked like a white horse with golden ears.

Kingu and other "orbiting objects" made the chunk's shape continuously change. It would be hard to believe that this "intruder" is not the origin of the serpent and dragon myths, legends, and stories.

The most likely path of the mass of materials can be determined by careful studies of the still existing impact craters and debris deposits.

The combined mass of the remaining parts of Tiamat and the chunk would have been much larger than the Earth. Since the Earth did not totally disintegrate, it has been calculated that most of the great mass passed no closer than about 60,000 miles from Earth.

This mass was at least 350 times larger than our moon, and probably 4 times as close, making it appear to be 1400 times the size of the moon! And because of the energy from the supernova, its several impacts, and its very close approach, it appeared to be glowing brighter than the sun!

Even at a distance of 60,000 miles, its view would have spanned from horizon to horizon!

Chapter 4
Chaos on Earth

It is a great philosophical breakthrough for geologists to accept catastrophe as a normal part of Earth history. **Erie Kauffman**

These materials created the greatest chaos that mankind has ever experienced.

The First Winds

As the materials approached Earth, Earth's atmosphere began to be pulled by gravity towards the large stream of the spiraling material. These materials were more than 50 times the size of the Earth, most however, got no closer than 60,000 miles.

The winds continuously increased until they reached super-hurricane force.

The winds were initially strongest over the North American Continent because of the angle of approach, i.e. from northwest to southeast, first nearing Earth on the northwest corner of the North American Continent. But all of Earth experienced strong winds. These winds caused damages many times greater than the damage we experience from our strongest hurricanes and tornados of today.

They eventually built up to intensities strong enough to sweep most surface materials into violent debris clouds and redeposit some of them hundreds of miles from their original positions. These new deposits also contained materials from the chunk and from Tiamat.

Trees were pulled up by the roots and strewn many miles away. Entire forests were swept away.

The winds eroded away sand and earthen hills down to base rock. Sand and grit in the winds polished rocks, and in some cases also eroded them away.

Even large boulders were blown miles from their normal positions.

The Mayans named these severe winds after their god Hurakan. A corruption of this name became hurricane.

The Mesopotamians said that their god: **"Marduk created the evil wind, and tempest, and the hurricane, and the fourfold wind, and the sevenfold wind, and the whirlwind, and the wind which has no equal."**

The violent winds made extremely loud noises. North American Indians remember a monster with a whistle in his mouth.

The Electromagnetic Discharges

Enormous electromagnetic discharges flashed between Earth and the various components of the swarm of materials from Tiamat and the chunk. These discharges became ever more violent as the materials approached nearer to Earth. The severe lighting and unbelievable noise sent many scurrying to caves, rocks, and other possible shelters. This may have been the major warning that most people received, and may have resulted in more people being saved than did any other factor.

These ever-increasing discharges created great heat.

Heat and Evaporation

The lakes and rivers began to evaporate. The seas steamed. This added to the imbalance in electromagnetic charge, and caused the discharges to continue, creating even more heat.

Remember the Biblical passages about the river evaporations that I asked you to remember earlier?

The heat became enormous. All shallow rivers and lakes evaporated completely. The seas and oceans continued to steam and parts of them boiled away.

The Earth's surface was heated to such a degree that water within rocks exploded the rocks, adding to the swirling debris.

Fires and Debris

Grasses, trees, and other combustibles burst into flame, starting many great fires. This, added to the velocity of the great winds, created super-hurricane firestorm intensities on various parts of Earth.

The great winds swept up great qualities of dust, vegetation, dirt, and even large rocks, and carried them in scouring debris over much of the Earth. We can still see where debris of various types filled valleys and depressions and piled drifts across the countryside.

The combustible materials, blowing in the great hurricanes, fed the fires causing them to burn much of everything encountered.

Crust Fractures and Earthquakes

The gravitational tidal waves within the Earth caused by the close approach of Tiamat and the chunk, resulted in great fractures in the Earth's crust. The great tectonic plates broke into more pieces.

Earthquakes occurred all over the where.

Thousands of volcanoes erupted, spewing rocks, dust, smoke, and lava into the building chaos. These materials began to rain down on the surface in depths of thousands of feet in some places.

Great avalanches of sand, dirt, and rock raced across the land at over 200 miles per hour. Tsunamis raced across the seas and upon parts of the land at over 500 miles per hour.

Escaping gases ignited, adding to the great fires.

Boiling hot steam, filled with grit, sprayed about the areas, "polishing" stones and destroying most materials in their paths.

Boiling mud and mudslides flowed into many depressions.

Lava and magma flowed liberally.

The Earth's poles flipped and reversed the magnetic charges, creating even more heat. The firestorms were intensified. Now all of the seas began to boil, further evaporating.

The cracks in the Earth's crust became more numerous, and larger. The tectonic plates fractured more and moved independently of each other, thrusting up great mountains and sinking great landmasses.

Areas in the Himalayan Mountains and in the Alps were thrust up an additional 6,000 feet. Mountains in China (Bayuan Kara Shan) were thrust up an additional 6,500 feet. The Sierra Nevada and Cascades in California and Oregon also gained heights of an additional 6,500 feet. The Tibetan Plateau increased elevations by 9,750 feet. Alpine peaks increased by 13,000 feet, as did the Andes.

The Rockies were thrust eastward by 8 miles.

And great areas sank, replacing the material that had been thrust up in the increased elevations. Extremely large landmasses in the Pacific Ocean sank. The floor of the North Atlantic Ocean sank over 9,000 feet. The land about the Azores, which, according to Plato, may have been Atlantis, sank almost 3 miles.

Great fords were opened in the Scandinavian areas. The Gobi Desert changed from a lake to a dry plain that later became a desert. Some of the great ancient rivers of India disappeared.

Almost the entire surface of the Earth was changed.

The atmosphere became saturated with smoke, dust, water vapor, and debris. This further intensified the discharges between Earth, Earth's atmosphere, and the various bodies still approaching Earth.

And the heat was even further intensified. Most of the small seas evaporated completely, and much of the oceans boiled away.

The heat was far too great for any of the water vapor to condense to form rain.

Some of the cracks in the Earth's crust opened further, swallowing everything nearby. Some shifted; then closed on their swallowed materials. Some stayed open and became the great fords and locks we still have today.

Many of the volcanic eruptions and Earthquakes could be felt 1000 miles away. All of the Earth trembled with shocks and reverberating aftershocks.

And some of the seismic activity started then is still tailing off today.

Great Ocean Waves Form

The great mass of Tiamat and the chunk continued towards Earth.

Water remaining in the oceans was drawn into a pile towards the great approaching masses to form a water thickness many miles high. It tended to follow the stream of materials as the materials passed close to Earth's surface. But the water could not move fast enough to follow. It continued to pile up until the stream of masses passed.

Earth Impacts

The spirally orbiting Kingu came within Earth's Roche Zone, i.e. within 8 to 12 thousands miles of Earth. The gravitational tidal waves caused Kingu to explode. It broke into three major chunks and millions of smaller pieces. At least two of the large pieces and at least a million of the smaller pieces fell to Earth. Some pieces continued on with the great mass of Tiamat and the chunk. Some scattered and became meteors and asteroids.

Millions of pieces of Kingu, Tiamat, and the chunk impacted the Earth and formed the Carolina Bays and similar craters still visible today.

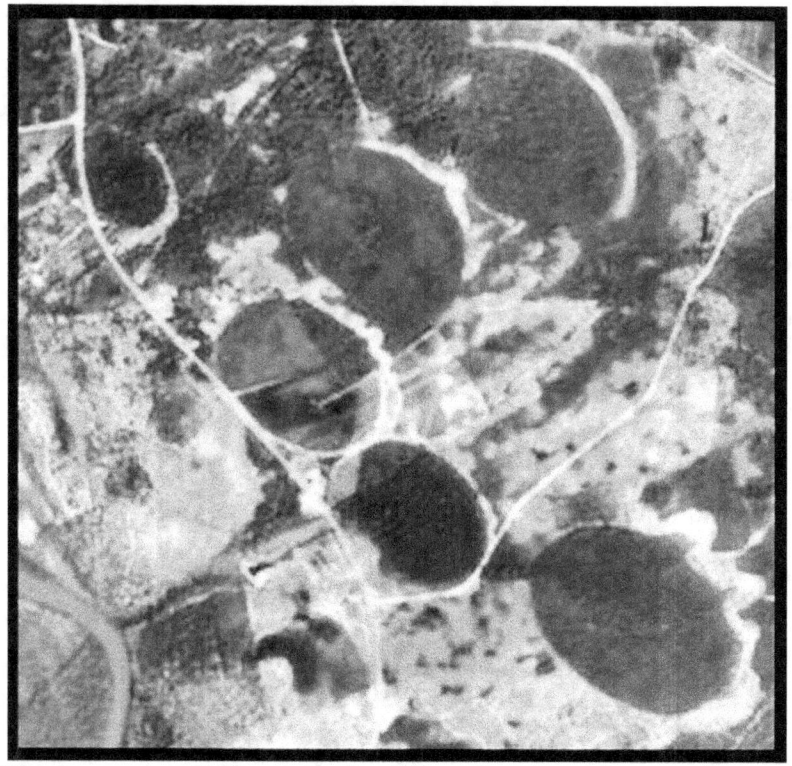

The impacts of Kingu in the "Carolina Bays" are still very visible.

Two very large pieces fell into the ocean east of the Carolinas and formed the large craters still visible in the Atlantic Ocean.

Rains of gravel-like stones and various types of debris fell on much of the Earth.

All of this activity added even more heat.

We can trace the path of the materials across Earth from the debris deposited by this mass of materials, from the impacts on Earth and from the displacements of Earth's features.

Great Waves Wash Over The Land

Earth's moon is drawn towards the mass and pulled into a wider orbit.

The rest of the great masses whizzed on past Earth, headed towards a collision with the sun.

The pile of waters of the oceans collapsed and sent great waves, some initially over 3 miles high, over all landmasses except for the highest mountains, after the stream of materials had passed.

Great whales and other sea animals were washed hundreds of feet above sea level and deposited in cracks and depressions far inland. Archeological finds prove that the great waves were at least 1500 feet above the land even hundreds of miles inland.

The great waves continued to sweep across the face of the Earth until they finally, after several cycles, wore themselves down to "ripples" that remained contained within the ocean basins.

The waves extinguished most of the fires, but the heat was still far too great for the evaporated water to condense and fall as rain.

Darkness

Thousands of volcanoes continued to pour smoke and debris into the water vapor loaded atmosphere. The resulting debris cloud totally blocked out the sun, the moon and all stars.

The blackness lasted for years.

The Central American Aztecs say: **"After the destruction of the fourth sun, the world plunged into darkness during the space of twenty-five years."**

Analyzing data from volcanoes over the last few hundred years, suggests that total blackness probably lasted for at least 3 years, as stated in ancient Russian literature. When some light did return, the American Indian legends state that: **"... the light was quite as scanty as it had been down below (in the caves where** they had escaped the disaster), for there was as yet no heaven, no sun, nor moon, nor stars."

It is likely that, even after the 3 years, it took several more decades before the sun light returned to near the conditions of today.

Gradual Cooling

Gradually the enormous heat dissipated as it radiated from the tops of the clouds at a greater rate than heat could be absorbed from the blocked sun. The water vapor condensed and it finally began to rain.

It wasn't too long before the rains had increased to extremely hard downpours.

And the great flood of legend really did happen.

The Flood

It has been calculated that more than half of all waters on Earth had evaporated and formed "the canopy" of debris laden clouds that blacked out the sun. It is likely that additional waters were also brought to Earth by "debris" from Tiamat.

When it finally began to cool enough for the water vapor to condense, the clouds would have been very heavy all the way down to the ground; giving rise to the "collapsed sky" stories found in most of the descriptions of the time.

It is easy to believe that it then rained for "forty days and forty nights" as stated in the Bible.

This very heavy downpour that lasted for a very long period, which followed the great waves that washed across the land, is the firm foundation for the many legends of the worldwide flood.

The Bitter Cold

The imbalance in heat radiated, versus heat absorbed, increased exponentially such that it reached the point where it almost suddenly got very cold.

As the rate of cooling became faster, the rain turned to sleet, hail, and snow. Everything became blackened from the great masses of debris in the clouds.

Most of the Earth became bitter cold. And it remained bitter cold and very dark for years.

Return of The Sun

Finally most of the water vapor in the clouds condensed and fell as snow and some of the debris was washed from the clouds.

The sun begins to show through the still debris-laden clouds.

Gradually it begins to get warmer. The snows and ice begin to melt and cause additional floods. These secondary flooding conditions continued for over a year.

And it was decades before the skies were completely clear of all the debris from the disaster and from the volcanoes that continued to erupt.

Earth's climate has not yet, after 11,500 years, returned to the pre-disaster norm of the Golden Age.

The disaster destroyed almost all life of all kinds. The face and internal structure of the Earth was changed forever.

But some humans did survive, and they recorded their memories.

Chapter 5
Ancient Documentation

"The trouble with the world is not that people know too little, but that they know so many things that ain't so." Mark Twain

Many elements of this great disaster have been recorded down through the ages. Some have been memorialized in great literature. A major problem, of course, is that the literature has been copied, and edited, perhaps unconsciously, down through the ages. Later scribes and copiers, who did not witness the events, have created significant alterations. We must keep this in mind as we review the ancient documents.

Sumerian Enuma Elish: Marduk

One of the oldest written records of the disaster was found in an ancient library in Nineveh. When archeologists excavated this library of King Assurbanipal, they found the first tablets dating back to about 650 BC, but it was acknowledged in the tablets that they had been copied from a much older text.

Later excavations in ancient Sumer found incomplete clay tablet fragments that told essentially the same story. Piecing them together, they were able to translate The Enuma Elish of ancient Sumer.

The Enuma Elish consists of seven clay tablets plus various fragments. It is a very repetitive document. This repetitiveness and some additional lines have been omitted for the sake of brevity, but otherwise the translations given here are word for word.

One of the several clay tablets of the Enuma Elish.

The Enuma Elish has erroneously been referred to as "The Epic of Creation", but as noted by translator L. W. King, the epic "took place after men had been created and cities had been built."

In a manner, however it is an epic of creation in that life on Earth had to be re-created after the great disaster.

There have been several slightly varying translations of the Enuma Elish. Here is presented the basic story, with word for word quotes from some of the translations.

The first tablet describes the gods fear that their mother, Tiamat, is plotting war against some of the other gods. It is believed that Tiamat was considered to be the mother of the gods because she

50

was, at the time, the brightest object in the heavens, except for the sun and moon.

The other gods try to dissuade her, but to no avail. So they call upon a new god, Marduk.

Here we see that Marduk is the Sumerian name for the chunk of materials, just as Satan is the Hebrew name.

"In the Chamber of Fates, the place of Destinies,

A god was engendered, most able and wisest of gods;

In the heart of the Deep was Marduk created."

That is, Marduk came from outer space in accordance with the description of the exploding star Vela described above. He could be seen from Earth because he was glowing hot from Vela's supernova and from probable encounters with bodies in the Kuiper Belt and encounters with some of the planets.

"Alluring was his figure,

Sparkling the lift of his eyes;

Lordly was his gait (orbit), commanding as of olden times....

Greatly exalted was he above the gods, exceeding throughout....

His members were enormous, he was exceeding tall....

When he moved his lips fire blazed forth."

A separate tablet fragment further describes his size:

"Fifty kaspu (about 350 miles) in his length,

One kaspu (about 6.5 miles) in his height,

Six cubits (about 9 feet) in his mouth,

Twelve cubits (about 18 feet) his...."

Here the text is lost.

When he entered the solar system, the planets:

".... Heaped upon him their awesome flashes.... (and he became) clothed with the halo of ten gods."

This is believed to describe the enormous exchanges of electromagnetic charges between Marduk and the planets, which caused Marduk to glow even brighter; ten times brighter than a normal god (planet).

Marduk continued into the solar system, passing Neptune and Uranus, which:

"Heaped upon him their awesome flashes...."

Marduk is "glorified" with electromagnetic flashes.

Then he approached Saturn:

"And he drew nigh and stood before Ansar (Saturn).

Ansar beheld him and his heart was filled with joy,

He kissed him on the lips and his fear departed from him."

And Saturn praises Marduk.

"O my son, who knoweth all wisdom,

....speedily set out upon thy way...."

And Marduk takes this opportunity to ask:

"If I, your avenger,

Conquer Tiamat and save your lives,

Appoint an assembly to proclaim my destiny supreme."

"Ansar (Saturn) opened his mouth,

And unto Gaga (a moon of Saturn), his minister, spake the word,

"O Gaga, thou minister that rejoices my spirits, unto Lahmu (Mars) and Lahamu (Venus) will I send thee."

Saturn instructs Gaga to go tell the other gods, and:

"Make ready; for a feast, at a banquet let them sit...."

Saturn's moon Gaga (today's Chiron) is released from its orbit around Saturn, and injected into its own orbit around the sun, as previously described.

And Marduk approaches Tiamat.

"Go, and cut off the life of Tiamat,

And let the wind carry her blood into secret places."

That is, parts of her are to be scattered into unknown space.

And Marduk proceeded.

"He set the lighting in front of him,

With burning flame he filled his body.

He made a net to enclose the inward parts of Tiamat..."

Marduk and Tiamat exchange electromagnetic charges. Their gravities act as nets to attract each other.

As Marduk gets closer, Tiamat's moon, Kingu, is pulled from its orbit and attracted to Marduk.

"The Lord (Marduk) drew nigh,

He gazed upon the inward parts of Tiamat,

He perceived the muttering of Kingu, her spouse.

As Marduk gazed, Kingu was troubled in his gait (orbit),

His will was destroyed and his (regular) motions ceased."

And Marduk says:

"Stand! I and thou, let us join in battle!"

"When Tiamat heard these words,

She was like one possessed,

She lost her reason."

"Tiamat uttered wild, piercing cries,

She trembled and shook to her very foundations."

"Tiamat and Marduk, the wisest of gods, advanced against one another;

They pressed on to single combat, they approached for battle."

This describes the extremely violent electromagnetic discharges between the two bodies as they got closer and closer. It produced great heat and thunderous acoustics that could even be heard on Earth.

And the battle rages:

"The Lord (Marduk) spread out his net and caught her;"

"The Evil Wind that was behind him he let loose in her face."

"As she opened her mouth, Tiamat, to devour him –

He drove the Evil Wind so that she closed not her lips.

The Fierce Storm Winds then filled her belly.

And her courage was taken from her,

And her mouth she opened wide.

He shot there through an arrow,

It tore her belly,

It cut through her insides,

Tore into her womb.

Having thus subdued her, her life breath he extinguished."

Tiamat is torn to pieces.

The "Evil Wind", the "Fierce Storm Winds", and the "arrow" were parts of the trail of materials following the chunk as previously described.

The gravitational tides caused the surface of Tiamat to crack, "open her mouth", and the various materials impacted with Tiamat.

This is the almost unbelievable written account of the destruction of the great planet, Tiamat!

Marduk tore Tiamat apart and:

"And caused the North Wind to bear it to places that have been unknown."

That is, outer space. And other pieces of her he:

"Locking them together, as watchmen he stationed them...

He bent Tiamat's tail to form the Great Band as a bracelet."

The explosion of the impact, coupled with the even more violent electromagnet discharges and gravitational interactions, spread much of the materials into "the Great Band as a bracelet." That is, the asteroid belt, which now occupies the previous, but wider orbit of Tiamat.

But much of the resulting material followed Marduk:

"The gods, her helpers who marched at her side...

Found themselves ensnared...."

"He took them captive, he broke their weapons;

In the net they were caught and in the snare they sat down....

They were held in bondage."

The remaining material followed Marduk on his path towards the sun. And as for Tiamat's moon, Kingu:

"He took from him the Tablets of Destiny....

He sealed them with a seal and in his own breast he laid them."

That is, Marduk changed Kingu's orbit. The Tablets of Destiny have been determined to mean the fixed destiny of a fixed patrol, or orbit.

Kingu now followed Marduk in a corkscrew type orbit as previously described.

And so the great planet Tiamat was removed from the heavens, never to be seen again.

And Marduk?

We know that Marduk, the celestial chunk, then disturbed and passed Earth and went on to impact the sun.

But:

"He conquered Tiamat,

He troubled and ended her life,

In the future of mankind,

When the days grow old,

May this be heard without ceasing;

May it hold sway forever!"

And thus Marduk became the principle god of Sumer.

Sumerian Ziusudra Warning of Flood

The Sumerians also have a story of being warned about the flood coming.

There are several ancient documented stories of the flood, and hundreds of oral versions. The story of Noah's flood is perhaps the best known. However it is generally agreed that the story of Ziusudra of ancient Mesopotamia is the oldest written version of the flood warning.

The ancient clay tablets tell how human noise vexed the chief god Enlil so much that he persuaded the divine assembly to vote for the destruction of man by sending a flood.

At that time, Ziusudra was king and lustration priest. He fashioned, being a seer, the god of giddiness and stood in awe beside it, wording his wishes humbly.

As he stood there regularly day after day something that was not a dream was appearing: Conversation.

A swearing of oaths by heaven and Earth, A touching of throats.

And the gods bringing their thwarts up to Kiur.

And as Ziusudra stood there beside it, he went on hearing:

Step up to the wall to my left and listen! Let me speak a word to you at the wall and may you grasp what I say, may you heed my advice!

By our hand a flood will sweep over the cities of the half-bushel baskets, and the country;

The decision, that mankind is to be destroyed has been made. A verdict, a command of the assembly cannot be revoked,

An order of An and Enlil is not known ever to have been countermanded,

Their kingship, their term, has been uprooted, They must bethink themselves of that.

Now...

What I have to say to you...

Here the text has been lost, but other fragments suggest that the lost text instructed Ziusudra to build a chest (boat) to survive the flood. Then:

All the evil winds, all stormy winds gathered into one, And with them, then, the flood was sweeping over the cities of the half-bushel baskets for seven days and seven nights.

After the flood had swept over the country, after the evil wind had tossed the big boat about on the great waters, the sun came out spreading light over heaven and Earth.

Ziusudra then drilled an opening in the big boat.

And the gallant Utu (sun) sent his light into the interior of the big boat.

Ziusudra, being king, stepped up before Utu kissing the ground before him.

The king was butchering oxen, was being lavish with the sheep

Barley cakes, crescents together with...

...he was crumbling for him juniper, the pure plant of the mountains, he filled on the fire and with a ...clasped to the breast he...

Here the text is lost. Then:

He will disembark the small animals that come up from the Earth!

Ziusudra, being king, stepped up before An and Enlil kissing the ground.

And An and Enlil after honoring him were granting him life like a god's, were making lasting breath of life, like a god's, descend into him.

That day they made Ziusudra, preserver, as king, of the name of the small animals and the seed of mankind, live toward the east over the mountains in mount Dilmun.

We see the great similarities between this very much earlier version of the flood warning and the Hebrew version of Noah's flood.

India's Rig Veda: Indra

We first learn of Indra from the earliest Hindu writings in their ancient Rig Veda. Indra is the ruler of the Hindu gods as Zeus is the ruler of the Greek gods and Thor the ruler of the German gods.

Indra was the god of both rain and war. Indra's main weapon was the thunderbolt.

People worshipped Indra by sacrificing animals to him. But by around 300 BC the people didn't want to sacrifice animals so they gradually stopped worshipping Indra as their principal god. Instead they began to worship the new gods Shiva and Vishnu who didn't need animal sacrifices. But Indra remained a god and stories continued to be told about him.

It is almost certain that the Rig Veda of ancient India was copied from earlier documents.

The Rig Veda tells of the battle between the great god Indra and the mighty serpent Vritra.

Vritra had stolen water from the Earth. This is most likely the memory of the great evaporation period when the supernova materials was approaching Earth.

Indra rode forth to do battle with Vritra. After a long battle, Indra destroyed Vritra and slit him open. Great floods of water fell from the skies. Indra became the chief god of ancient India.

Indra

It is interesting to note that Indra's heaven was in the clouds above the sacred mountain Meru. This is the same mountain associated with Atlantis.

From the Rigveda we read that the gods realized that they could not hold their power until Vritra was destroyed. This is almost certainly an echo of the same message from the gods described in the Enuma Elish. The gods had the artisan god, Twashtri prepare a weapon for Indra. Twashtri built the weapon and spoke to Indra:

"With this, the best of weapons, O exalted one, reduce that fierce foe of the gods to ashes! And, having slain the foe, rule thou happily the entire domain of heaven, O chief of the celestials, with those that follow thee."

Indra heads into battle and finds that Vritra is surrounded by Danavas (demons) that look like great mountain peaks. The battle ensues, with Indra first attacking the horde of Danavas. Indra drove them into the sea. Indra then kills Vritra.

I have slain Vritra, O ye hast'ning Maruts;

I have grown mighty through my own great vigor;

I am the hurler of the bolt of Thunder –

For man flow freely now the gleaming waters.

Then on Earth his worshippers praised him:

I will extol the manly deeds of Indra;

The first was when the Thunder stone he wielded And smote the Dragon; he released the waters,

He opened the channels of the breasted mountains.

He smote the Dragon Vritra in its fortress.

Twashtri had shaped for him the thunder weapon –

Then rushing freely like to bellowing castle, The gladsome waters to the sea descended.

The smitten monster fell amidst the torrents,

That pause nor stay, forever surging onward;

Then Vritra covered by the joyful billows Was carried to the darksome deeps of Ocean.

This does indeed sound like a simplified revision of the Enuma Elish, perhaps written several centuries later, and incorporating ancient India's principal god.

Norse Poetic Edda: The Serpent

The Norse Eddas are considered to be among the greatest of the world's literature. Most were written about 1000 years ago, but it is clear they were taken from very ancient literature. One of their great stories seems to parallel other stories of the great disaster.

Norse Poetic Edda: The Serpent

For the sake of brevity, only excerpts are given here:

The war I remember, the first in the world,

When the gods with spears had smitten Gollveig,

And in the hall of Hor had burned her,

Three times burned, and three times born,

Oft and again, yet ever she lives.

Here Gollveig has been interpreted as "the one who refines gold by fire", and Hor "the High One".

Yggdrasil shakes, and shiver on high

The ancient limbs, and the giant is loose;

To the head of Mim does Othin give heed

But the kinsman of Surt shall slay him soon.

Yggdrasil is the axis of the Earth. The head of Mim is the severed head of a water god that can talk and give advice to Othin. Othin is the chief of the gods. Surt is the giant who rules the fire-world.

Against the serpent goes Othin's son.

The sun turns black, Earth sinks in the sea,

The hot stars down from heaven are whirled;

Fierce grows the steam and life-feeding flame,

Till fire leaps high about heaven itself.

This is a quite precise description of what happened in the disaster!

The poem then tells that the sun came back and everything became good again.

Norse Elder Edda: Fenris-Wolf and Midgard-Serpent

Another version in the Eddas tells:

Then it shall come to pass that the Earth will shake so violently

That the trees will be torn up by the roots,

The mountains will topple down,

And all bonds and fetters will be broken and snapped.

The Fenris-wolf (one of the fragments) gets loose.

The sea rushes over the Earth,

For the Midgard-serpent (another fragment) writhes in giant rage,

And seeks to gain the land.

It would be hard to believe that these are not describing the great disaster, rewritten many centuries later in terms of the gods of the ancient Norse.

Norse Edda: Bitter Cold

After describing the great disaster in terms of the war in heaven as presented above, and then the flood as also described above, the Eddas then speak of the bitter cold.

First there is a winter called the Fimbuyl winter, the mighty; the great, the iron winter, when snow drives from all quarters, the frosts are so severe, the winds so keen, that there is no joy in the sun. There are three such winters in succession, without any intervening summer.

.... As soon as the streams that.... (flow under the ice) had come so far.... (they).... turned into ice. And when this ice stopped and flowed no more, then gathered over it the drizzling rain.... And froze into rime, and one layer of ice was laid upon another clear into (their land) and all of (their land) was filled with thick and heavy ice and rime, and everywhere were drizzling rain and gusts.

Their literature speaks of severe, bitter cold that lasted for three years. It is interested to note that Russian literature also state that the winter lasted three years.

Persia's Tistrya

Avestic scriptures of ancient Persia tell of the Evil One, Angra Mainyu that created a mighty serpent called Tistrya that assaulted and deranged the sky and sent snow and vehement destroying frost. The gods warned Yima that this was going to happen.

Tistrya was called "The leader of the stars against the planets."

Persia's Yima: Bitter Cold

Ancient Persia also has a story almost identical to the Norse in their literature. It appears that both are from the same, ancient source.

Mexican Aztecs: Bitter Cold

The Aztecs of Mexico also remember the time of bitter cold, as indicated in their ancient prayer.

Know, O Lord…. The men have no garments, nor the women, to cover themselves…. With great toil and weariness they scrape together enough for each day, going by mountain and wilderness seeking their food; so faint and enfeebled are they that their bowels cleave to their ribs, and; all their body re-echoes with hollowness…. They tremble with cold, and for leanness they stagger in walking….. Though they stay by a fire, they find little heat.

Egypt's Osiris

Egypt has a similar story of a fight between Osiris the sun god and Set the evil one. Set wins and cuts Osiris's body into 14 parts and scatters them about the Earth.

Osiris's consort, wife and sister, finds the parts and helps resurrect Osiris in the form of his son Horus.

The basic belief at this time is that ancient Egypt worshipped the sun god Osiris. When the evil one, Set, destroyed the sun, i.e. when it did not shine for a few years, they postulated that Osiris was now a dead god, and therefore God of the Dead. He was resurrected in the form of his son Horus when the sun reappeared. But he himself also remained as the god of the dead.

Greece's Typhon

The Greek also had a similar story. Their chief god Zeus battles Typhon. Typhon has been described as the largest and ugliest monster ever born. He had a hundred horrible heads that touched the stars. Lava and red-hot stones poured from his gaping mouths. He hissed like a hundred snakes and roared like a hundred lions. He tore up whole mountains and threw them at the gods.

Zeus engaged him in a terrible battle and was defeated. Typhon cut out Zeus' tendons and hid them. Zeus' son is able to return the tendons and repairs Zeus, who returns to an even more heated battle that destroyed almost all living creatures on Earth.

When Typhon tore up the huge Mont Aetna to hurl at the gods, Zeus struck Typhon with a hundred thunderbolts and the mountain fell back, pinning Typhon beneath.

Typhon is still there, and that's why Aetna still belches fire, lava, and smoke to this day.

Aetna

Typhon cutting out Zeus' tendons may be analogous to Set dismembering Osiris. More likely both stories came from a single, more ancient source.

Greece: Homer's Iliad

Homer, sometime before 800 BC, wrote his famous Iliad. It seems clear that he took materials from a very ancient version of the great disaster.

... Zeus, from the top of many-deled Olympus, bade Themis gather the gods in council, where on she went about and called them to the house of Zeus."

Poseidon

Why, wielder of the lighting, have you called the gods to council?

Zeus

You know my purpose, shaker of Earth and wherefore I have called you hither.

Zeus gave the word for war.

Poseidon shook the vast Earth, and bade the high hills tremble.

Hades, King of the realms below was struck with fear; he sprang panic-stricken from his throne and cried aloud in terror lest Poseidon, lord of the Earthquake, should crack the ground over his head, and lay bare his moldy mansions to the sight of mortals and immortals, mansions so ghastly grim that even the gods shudder to think of them.

Homer frequently refers to Poseidon as: "Earth-encircling Poseidon", and states:

Forthwith he shed a darkness before the eyes of the son of Peleus,....

Peleus was a mortal wedded to Thetas, a sea nymph. Her son was Achilles, the key hero of Iliad.

This may refer to the darkness caused by the cloud of the disaster.

Later Homer tells of the darkness being removed from Achilles eyes.

The author believes that several ancient documents and rewrites thereof existed in Homer's time. And just as various scribes, et al rewrote some of these, as well documented in the clay tablets of Sumer and Babylon, so Homer may have done some rewriting.

Unfortunately, most of the ancient records available in Homer's time were destroyed with the destruction of the great library in Alexandria.

Greek Deucalion's Flood

In Greek mythology, the supreme god Zeus decides to destroy mankind because they were disrespectful and sinful. Prometheus, a man that benefits men (a priest?), warns his son Deucalion that the gods Zeus and Poseidon are going to cause a flood. He tells him to build a boat.

The Greek Apollodorus gives this version:

And Prometheus had a son Deucalion. He reigning in the regions about Phthia, married Phyrra, the daughter of Epimetheus and Pandora, the first woman fashioned by the Gods.

And when Zeus would destroy the men of the Bronze Age, Deucalion by the advice of Prometheus constructed a chest, and having stored it with provisions he embarked in it with Pyrrha.

But Zeus by pouring heavy rain from heaven flooded the greater part of Greece, so that all men were destroyed, except a few who fled to the high mountains in the neighborhood.

It was there that the mountains in Thessaly parted, and that all the world outside the Isthmus and Peloponnese was overwhelmed. But Deucalion, floating in the chest

over the sea for nine days and as many nights, drifted to Parnassus, and there, when the rain ceased, he landed and sacrificed to Zeus, the god of Escape.

Deucalion's Flood, Ovid's Version

Ovid, the great Roman writer, later gave his version. Only limited excerpts are given for brevity.

Jove standing up aloft and leaning on his ivory Mace,

Right dreadfully his bushy locks did thrice or four times shake,

Wherewith he made both Sea and Land and Heaven it self to quake.

This basically agrees with the other stories that there were Earthquakes preceding the flood.

I must destroy both man and beast and all the mortal kind.

The man that had so traitorously against their Lord conspired.

That all had sworn and sold themselves to mischief us to grieve.

And therefore as they all offend: so am I fully bent,

That all forthwith (as they deserve) shall have due punishment.

So Zeus decides to destroy man, and some of the other gods agreed.

These words of Jove some of the Gods did openly approve,

And with their sayings more to wrath his angry courage move.

And some did give assent by signs. Yet did it grieve them all

That such destruction utterly on all mankind should fall,

To savage beasts to waste and spoil, because of mans offence.

The king of Gods bade cease their thought and questions in that case,

And cast the care thereof on him.

The beasts are also destroyed – because of man's offenses.

Zeus first thinks to destroy with fire, but reconsiders for the following reasons.

And now his lightning had he thought on all the Earth to throw,

But that he feared lest the flames perhaps so high should grow ...

As for to set the Heaven on fire, and burn up all the sky.

Zeus also remembers as earlier prophesy, i.e. a "destiny" that is to come in the future, and therefore he cannot use fire as a destruction at this time.

He did remember furthermore how that by destiny

A certain time should one day come, wherein both Sea and Land

And Heaven itself should feel the force of Vulcan's scorching brand,

So that the huge and goodly work of all the world so wide

Should go to wreck, for doubt whereof forthwith he laid aside.

So Zeus decides to use a flood.

He did determine with himself the mortal kind to drown.

...

And to the Sea with flowing streams swollen above their banks,

One rolling in another neck, they rushed forth by ranks.

Himself with his threatened Mace, did lend the Earth a blow,

That made it shake and open ways for waters forth to flow.

Men, beasts, trees, corn, and with their gods were Churches washed away.

No difference was between the sea and ground,

For all was sea: there was no shore nor landing to be found.

Some climbed up to tops of hills, and some rowed to and fro

One over corn and tops of towns, whom waves did overwhelm.

The Sea nymphs wondered under waves the towns and groves to see,

And Dolphins played among the tops and boughs of every tree.

The grim and greedy Wolfe did swim among the silly sheep,

The Lion and the Tiger fierce were borne upon the deep.

The fleeting fowls long having sought for land to rest upon,

Into the Sea with weary wings were driven to fall anon.

Unwonted waves on highest tops of mountains did rebound.

The greatest part of men were drowned, and such as escaped the flood,

Forlorn with fasting overlong did die for want of food.

When at this hill (for yet the Sea had whelmed all beside)

Deucalion and his bedfellow, without all other guide,

Arrived in a little Bark immediately they went,

And to the Nymphs of Corycus with full devout intent

Did honor due, and to the Gods to whom that famous hill

Was sacred, and to Themis eke in whose most holy will

Consisted then the Oracles.

In all the world so round

A better nor more righteous man could never yet be found

Than was Deucalion, nor again a woman, maiden nor wife,

That feared God so much as she, nor led so good a life. ...

When Jove beheld how all the world stood like a plash of rain,

And of so many thousand men and women did remain

But one of each, howbeit those both just and both devout,

He brake the Clouds, and did command that Boreas with his stout

And sturdy blasts should chase the flood, that Earth might see the sky.

And swelling streams of flowing floods within her channels sank.

Then hills did rise above the waves that had them overflow,

And as the waters did decrease the ground did seem to grow.

The world restored was again, which though Deucalion rejoiced.

What very ancient sources did Ovid have? It certainly describes the flood and provides details not included in the other stories.

Such sources were most likely destroyed long ago. But, we may yet find them in some ancient lost library. We can only hope.

Rome's Metamorphoses by Ovid: Phaeton

One of history's most famous writers is the Roman Ovid, more formally known as Publius Ovidius Naso. He lived from 43 BC to 18 AD and wrote his Metamorphoses about 1 AD.

Book II of Metamorphoses is Ovid's description of Phaeton. It is a long and detailed story of how the Sun God let his son take the reins one day. This is Ovid's reasoning of how things went so awry and caused the great destruction. He obviously took much of his story from a more ancient document in that it closely relates to the more ancient documents described later.

Phaeton is the son of Apollo, i.e. the son of the sun. To prove this to his schoolmates, Phaeton asks to drive the sun's chariot for a day. His father responds:

Apollo

I beg you to withdraw this request. It is not a safe boon, nor one, my Phaeton, suited to your youth and strength. Your lot is mortal, and you ask what is beyond a mortal's power.

In your ignorance you aspire to do that which not even the gods themselves may do. None but myself may drive the flaming car of day. Not even Jupiter whose terrible right arm hurls the thunderbolts.

The first part of the way is steep, and such as the horses when fresh in the morning can hardly climb; the middle is high up in the heavens, whence I myself can scarcely, without alarm, look down and behold the Earth and sea stretched beneath me.

The last part of the road descends rapidly, and requires most careful driving.

Tethys, who is waiting to receive me, often trembles for me lest I should fall headlong. Add to all this, the heaven is all the time turning round and carrying the stars with it.

I have to be perpetually on my guard lest that movement, which sweeps everything else along, should hurry me also away.

Suppose I should lend you the chariot, what would you do? Could you keep your course while the sphere was revolving under you?

Perhaps you think that there are forests and cities, the abodes of gods, and palaces and temples on the way.

On the contrary, the road is through the midst of frightful monsters. You pass by the horns of the Bull, in front of the Archer, and near the Lion's jaws, and where the Scorpion stretches its arms in one direction and the Crab in another.

Nor will you find it easy to guide those horses, with their breasts full of fire that they breathe forth from their mouths and nostrils. I can scarcely govern them myself, when they are unruly and resist the reins.

Beware, my son, lest I be the donor of a fatal gift; recall your request while yet you may.

Do you ask me for a proof that you are sprung from my blood? I give you a proof in my fears for you. Look at my face, I would that you could look into my breast, you would there see all a father's anxiety.

Finally, he continued, look round the world and choose whatever you will of what Earth or sea contains most precious; ask it and fear no refusal.

This only I pray you not to urge. It is not honour, but destruction you seek.

Why do you hang round my neck and still entreat me? You shall have it if you persist; the oath is sworn and must be kept, but I beg you to choose more wisely."

He ended; but the youth rejected all admonition and held to his demand. So, having resisted as long as he could, Apollo at last led the way to where stood the lofty chariot.

It was of gold, the gift of Vulcan; the axle was of gold, the pole and wheels of gold, the spokes of silver. Along the seat were rows of chrysolites and diamonds, which reflected all around the brightness of the sun.

While the daring youth gazed in admiration, the early Dawn threw open the purple doors of the east, and showed the pathway strewn with roses. The stars withdrew, marshaled by the Daystar, which last of all retired also.

The father, when he saw the Earth beginning to glow, and the Moon preparing to retire, ordered the Hours to harness up the horses. They obeyed, and led forth from the lofty stalls the Steeds full fed with ambrosia, and attached the reins.

Then the father bathed the face of his son with a powerful unguent, and made him capable of enduring the brightness of the flame. He set the rays on his head, and, with a foreboding sigh, said:

Apollo

If, my son, you will in this at least heed my advice, spare the whip and hold tight the reins. They go fast enough of their own accord; the labour is to hold them in. You are not to take the straight road directly between the five circles, but turn off to the left. Keep within the limit of the middle zone, and avoid the northern and the southern alike.

You will see the marks of the northern and the southern alike. You will see the marks of the wheels, and they will serve to guide you. And, that the skies and the Earth may each receive their due share of heat, go not too high, or you will burn the heavenly dwellings, nor too low, or you will set the Earth on fire; the middle course is safest and best.

And now I leave you to your chance, which I hope will plan better for you than you have done for yourself.

Night is passing out of the western gates and we can delay no longer. Take the reins; but if at last your heart fails you, and you will benefit by my advice, stay where you are in safety, and suffer me to light and warm the Earth.

The agile youth, sprang into the chariot, stood erect, and grasped the reins with delight pouring out thanks to his reluctant parent.

Phaeton

Meanwhile the horses fill the air with their snorting and fiery breath, and stamp the ground impatient. Now the bars are let down, and the boundless plain of the universe lies open before them. They dart forward and cleave the opposing clouds, and outrun the morning breezes which started from the same eastern goal.

The steeds soon perceived that the load they drew was lighter than usual; and as a ship without ballast is tossed hither and thither on the sea, so the chariot, without its accustomed weight, was dashed about as if empty.

They rush headlong and leave the traveled road. He is alarmed, and knows not how to guide them; nor, if he knew, has he the power.

Then, for the first time, the Great and Little Bear were scorched with heat, and would fain, if it were possible, have plunged into the water; and the Serpent which lies coiled up round the north pole, torpid and harmless, grew warm, and with warmth felt its rage revive. Bootes, they say, fled away, though encumbered with his plough, and all unused to rapid motion.

When hapless Phaeton looked down upon the Earth, now spreading in vast extent beneath him, he grew pale and his knees shook with terror. In spite of the glare all around him, the sight of his eyes grew dim. He wished he had never touched his father's horses, never learned his parentage; never prevailed in his request.

He is borne along like a vessel that flies before a tempest, when the pilot can do no more and betakes himself to his prayers.

What shall he do? Much of the heavenly road is left behind, but more remains before. He turns his eyes from one direction to the other; now to the goal whence he began his course, now to the realms of sunset which he is not destined to reach. He loses his self-command, and knows not what to do; whether to draw tight the reins or throw them loose; he forgets the names of the horses.

He sees with terror the monstrous forms scattered over the surface of heaven. Here the Scorpion extended his two great arms, with his tail and crooked claws stretching over two signs of the zodiac. When the boy beheld him, reeking with poison and menacing with his fangs, his course failed, and the reins fell from his hands.

The horses, when they felt them loose on their backs, dashed headlong, and unrestrained went off into unknown regions of the sky, in among the stars, hurling the chariot over pathless places, now up in high heaven, now down almost to the Earth.

Allow me to insert that it is here that we see Ovid's description of the great disaster that we have been discussing.

The moon saw with astonishment her brother's chariot running beneath her own. The clouds begin to smoke, and the mountaintops take fire; the fields are parched with heat, the plants wither, the trees with their leafy branches burn, the harvest is ablaze!

But these are small things. Great cities perished, with their walls and towers; whole nations with their people were consumed to ashes! The forest-clad mountains burned, Athos and Taurus and Tmolus and OEte; Ida, once celebrated for fountains, but now all dry; the Muses' mountain Helicon, and Haemus; Aetna, with fires within and without, and Parnassus, with his two peaks, and Rhodope, forced at last to part with his snowy crown. Her cold climate was no protection to Scythia, Caucasus burned, and Ossa and Pindus, and, greater than both, Olympus; the Alps high in air, and the Apennines crowned with clouds.

Phaeton caused the great fires and destruction.

Then Phaeton beheld the world on fire, and felt the heat intolerable. The air he breathed was like the air of a furnace and full of burning ashes, and the smoke was of a pitchy darkness. He dashed forward he knew not whither.

Then, it is believed, the people of Ethiopia became black by the blood being forced so suddenly to the surface, and the Libyan Desert was dried up to the condition in which it remains to this day.

The Nymphs of the fountains, with disheveled hair, mourned their waters, nor were the rivers safe beneath their banks: Tanais smoked, and Caicus, Xanthus, and Meander, Babylonian Euphrates and Ganges, Tagus with golden sands, and Cayster where the swans resort.

Nile fled away and hid his head in the desert, and there it still remains concealed. Where he used to discharge his waters through seven mouths into the sea, there seven dry channels alone remained.

The Earth cracked open, and through the chinks light broke into Tartarus, and frightened the king of shadows and his queen. The sea shrank up. Where here before was water, it became a dry plain; and the mountains that lie beneath the waves lifted up their heads and became islands. The fishes sought the lowest depths, and the dolphins no longer ventured as usual to sport on the surface.

Even Nereus, and his wife Doris, with the Nereids, their daughters, sought the deepest caves for refuge.

Thrice Neptune essayed to raise his head above the surface, and thrice was driven back by the heat.

Earth, surrounded as she was by waters, yet with head and shoulders bare, screening her face with her hand, looked up to heaven, and with a husky voice called on Jupiter (Zeus):

Earth

"O ruler of the gods, if I have deserved this treatment, and it is your will that I perish with fire, why withhold your thunderbolts?

Let me at least fall by your hand. Is this the reward of my fertility, of my obedient service? Is it for this that I have supplied herbage for cattle and fruits for men, and frankincense for your altars?

But if I am unworthy of regard, what has my brother Ocean done to deserve such a fate? If neither of us can excite your pity, think, I pray you, of your own heaven, and behold how both the poles are smoking which sustain your palace, which must fall if they be destroyed.

Atlas faints and scarce holds up his burden. If sea, Earth, and heaven perish, we fall into ancient Chaos.

Atlas

Save what yet remains to us from the devouring flame. O, take thought for our deliverance in this awful moment!"

Thus spoke Earth, and overcome with heat and thirst, could say no more.

Then Jupiter omnipotent, calling to witness all the gods, including him who had lent the chariot, and showing them that all was lost unless some speedy remedy were applied, mounted the lofty tower from whence he diffuses clouds over the Earth, and hurls the forked lightnings.

But at that time not a cloud was to be found to interpose for a screen to Earth, nor was a shower remaining unexhausted. He thundered, and brandishing a lightning bolt in his right hand launched it against the charioteer, and struck him at the same moment from his seat and from existence!

Phaeton Falls

Phaeton, with his hair on fire, fell headlong, like a shooting star which marks the heavens with its brightness as it falls, and Eridanus, the great river, received him and cooled his burning frame.

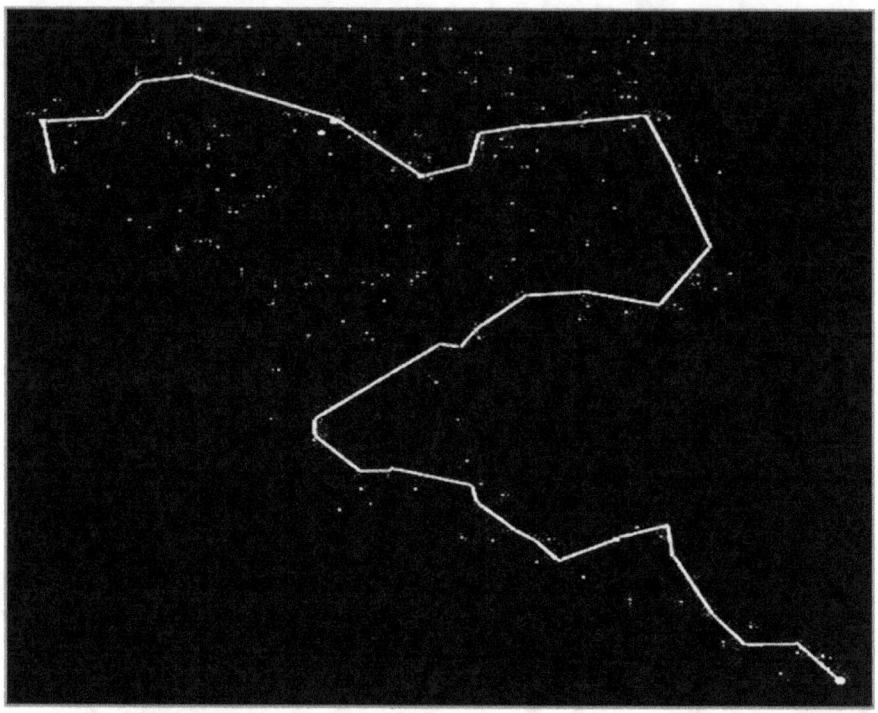

Eridanus, the great river is Pennsylvania's Constellation in the night sky that is named Eridanus.

The Italian Naiads reared a tomb for him, and inscribed these words upon the stone:

"Driver of Phoebus' (Apollo's) chariot, Phaeton,

Struck by Jove's thunder, rests beneath this stone.

He could not rule his father's car of fire,

Yet was it much so nobly to aspire."

We see that Ovid can be very flowery!

Hebrew's Satan

The Bible mentions Satan in many places. Perhaps the verses most closely related to the disaster story are from Revelation.

And I beheld when he had opened the sixth seal, and lo, there was a great Earthquake; and the sun became black as sackcloth of hair, and the moon became as blood; 6:12 And the stars of heaven fell unto the Earth.... Revelation 6:13

....And every mountain and island were moved out of their places. Revelation 6:14

And the Kings of the Earth, and .... (everyone) hid themselves in the dens and in the rocks of the mountains. Revelation 6:15

This sounds very much like the disaster previously described in scientific terms. And it appears in agreement with other "sacred texts" we have presented.

The War in Heaven

And there was a war in heaven; Michael and his angels fought against the dragon; and the dragon fought and his angels, Revelation 12:7

And prevailed not; neither was their place found any more in heaven. Revelation 12:8

And the great dragon was cast out, that old serpent, called the Devil, and Satan, which deceiveth the whole world; he was cast out into the Earth, and his angels were cast out with him. Revelation 12:9

This certainly sounds like a description of the disaster. And it may have been taken from earlier recorded documents that later became the Book of Job. It surely acknowledges who Satan is:

That old serpent, called the Devil, and Satan. Revelation 12:9

Isaiah also refers to the crooked serpent and tends to clarify the definition of the dragons and the leviathan.

In that day the Lord with his sore and great and strong sword shall punish leviathan the piercing serpent; even leviathan that crooked serpent; and He shall slay the dragon that is in the sea. Isaiah 27:1

Hebrew's Noah's Flood

The best-known story of the flood is the story of Noah in the Book of Genesis in the Bible.

And the Lord said, I will destroy man whom I have created from the face of the Earth; both man, and beast, and the creeping thing, and the fowls of the air; for it repenteth me that I have made them. Genesis 6:7

But Noah found grace in the eyes of the Lord. Genesis 6:8

And God said unto Noah, The end of all flesh is come before me; for the Earth is filled with violence through them; and, behold, I will destroy them with the Earth. Genesis 6:13

Make thee an ark of gopher wood; ... Genesis 6:14

In the six hundredth year of Noah's life, in the second month, the seventeenth day of the month, the same day were all the fountains of the great deep broken up, and the windows of heaven were opened. Genesis 7:11

And the rain was upon the Earth forty days and forty nights. Genesis 7:12

And the flood was forty days upon the Earth; and the waters increased, and bare up the ark, and it was lift up above the Earth. Genesis 7:17

And the waters prevailed upon the Earth an hundred and fifty days. Genesis 7:24

So Genesis tells us that God caused the flood. But Revelation has a different story.

And there was war in heaven; Michael and his angels fought against the dragon; and the dragon fought and his angels, Revelation 12:7

And prevailed not; neither was their place found any more in heaven. Revelation 12:8

And the great dragon was cast out, that old serpent, called the Devil, and Satan, which deceiveth the whole world: he was cast out into the Earth, and his angels were cast out with him. Revelation 12:9

Thus Revelation tells us that Satan was thrown to Earth and thereby caused the flood. Putting both stories together tells us that God caused the flood by throwing Satan to Earth.

American Ute's Ta-Wats

The Ute Indians of California remember when:

".... the sun was shivered into a thousand fragments, which fell to Earth causing a general conflagration."

Their hero of the disaster was Ta-Wats who:

".... Fled the burning Earth (that) consumed his feet, consumed his legs, consumed his body, consumed his hands and arms – all were consumed but the head alone, which bowled across valleys and over mountains, fleeing destruction from the burning Earth, until at last, swollen with heat, the eyes of .... (Ta-Wats) .... Burst and the tears gushed forth in a flood which spread over the Earth and extinguished the fire."

The Ute tribes of America have another story of the flood, indicating perhaps a separate memory.

(There was a war and).... The sun was shivered into a thousand fragments, which fell to Earth causing general conflagration. Then Ta-Wats fled before the destruction ... and as he fled the burning Earth consumed his feet, consumed his legs, consumed his body, consumed his hands and arms – all were consumed but the head alone, which bowled across valleys and over mountains, fleeing destruction from the burning Earth, until at last, swollen with heat, the eyes of ... Ta-Wats.... Burst and the tears gushed forth in a flood, which spread over the Earth and extinguished the fire.

Here again we have the same story elements:

1. War in heaven;

2. Sun shivered and falls to Earth;

3. Earth burns;

4. A flood puts out the fires.

Clearly this is just a different version of the same great disaster.

Summary of Memories of the Destruction

So we have many names for the chunk of materials that caused the great disaster, as summarized in the table.

Country	Chunk Name	Hero Name
Sumer	Marduk	Marduk
India	Vritra	Indra
Norse	Fenris-Wolf &	
	Midgard Serpent	Thor
	Hodur	Balder
Persia	Tistrya	
Egypt	Set (Seb)	Osiris
Greece	Typhon	Zeus
		Adonis
	Cacus	Hercules
Rome	Phaeton	
Hebrews	Satan	Jehovah
Brazil	Ariconte	Timandonar
Maya	Serpent Sky God	Hunab Ku
Ute	Ta-Wats	Ta-Wats

The Key Players in the Memories of the Disaster

Almost everyone recognized the chunk as a great, fiery serpent of some kind.

Most viewers, when they first saw the materials approaching initially thought that the intruder looked like a basic serpent.

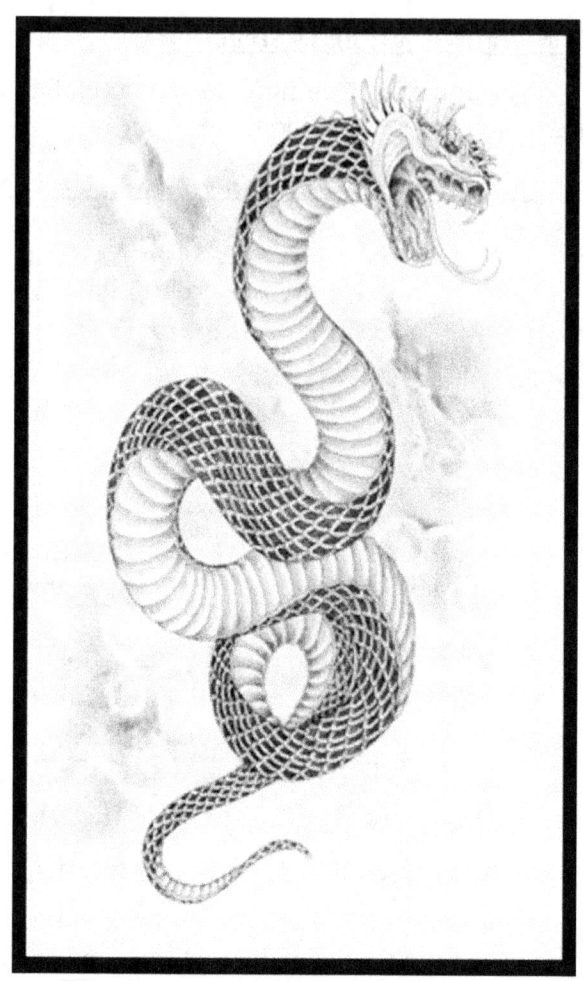

The Serpent Falling from Heaven

As it got closer it looked more like a multiple headed creature. Many thought that the debris surrounding it was a group of some sort of demons.

The Hydra Falling from Heaven

The hydra and the dragon were most likely based on memories of how the ancients described the cause of the destruction.

Dragon

Most of the "memories" are very similar. Only the Sumerians recognized the intruder as a good "god". This is because they made the villain to be the god Tiamat, which disappeared from the heavens.

And, in fact, most of the damage was done by pieces from Tiamat including her moon Kingu, which exploded and did the most damage.

The Norse had more than one version because it is believed that writers continued "editing" and changing the story even later than 1000 AD.

The Greeks also had several versions, as written by the great writers: Herodotus, Pliny and Strabo.

Other than the ancient Sumerians and Babylonians, most of the others recognized the intruder as an evil serpent, and this became the dominant belief. There can be little doubt that this intruder was the basis for Satan. Most still believe that Satan caused the disaster.

Ancient Beliefs for the Cause of the Disaster

It is also interesting to consider the various beliefs for the cause of the great disaster.

People	God	Cause	Hero
Sumer	Enki	Not Serving Gods	Ziusudra
Akkadian	Ea	Same	Uthnapishtim
Greece	Prometheus	Wickedness	Deucalion
Hebrew	Jehovah	Wickedness	Noah
Ute	No one	None	Ta-Wats
Norse			Thor
Persia	gods		Yima
Egypt	No one	None	Osiris

Summary Review of The Flood Stories

These disaster stories are generally considered to be the major ones. There are dozens more.

Conclusion

The worldwide literature is too consistent to be a coincidence. It seems quite clear that there was indeed a worldwide destruction that included a flood.

It also seems clear that many of the stories most likely derived from one or a few common stories of eyewitnesses.

John used details of these stories to write Revelation. It is not known exactly what John believed about these stories. Did he believe that they were revelations of the future given to him from God? Did he believe that the documentations he found were of actual events?

In any case he foretold that such an event would happen again and that it would begin the end times.

Revelation does indeed foretell that an asteroid or a similar heavenly body will destroy mankind on Earth.

Revelation is the story of our end.

Revelation's prediction is strongly supported by an ancient document written by eyewitnesses to the great disaster.

Chapter 6
Eyewitnesses to the Destruction

Oh that my words were written! Oh that they were printed in a book! **Job 19:23**

The Book of Job in the Bible is the world's oldest surviving document. Most scholars including Magee, Schultens, Lowth and Michaelis agree.

Job and the Chief Priest Eliphaz, and their companions were eyewitnesses to the great destruction and flood.

They watched as the alien materials approached. They ran to take shelter in a cave, but before they got inside Job was struck by burning embers that covered a large part of his body. His companions rushed him inside the cave and it was from the cave that the world's oldest surviving document was written as the eyewitness account of the disaster.

Being mankind's oldest available document, there have been many rewrites and interpretations. My interpretation provides three comparative sets of information:

1. The events as recorded in the Kings James version of the Bible;

2. The events as determined by the scientific evidence previously presented; and

3. My interpretation of the Bible's Book of Job in light of the scientific evidence.

I begin with Job 2:7 because key scholars agree that the first part of the Book of Job is very different than the basic story, and was clearly written much later than the body of the Book.

***

So went Satan forth from the presence of the Lord, and smote Job with sore boils from the sole of his foot unto his crown. Job 2:7.

Satan, the chunk of material from the supernova, left the heavens and rained hot rocks and sands upon Earth. Job and his companions had been watching the approaching fiery materials for many days. They had begun to experience the heavy winds caused by Satan pulling Earth's atmosphere towards it.

Job was outside a cave where they had gone to seek shelter. He was watching Satan when a great gust of wind bearing hot sands and dust, suddenly began to rain down upon him. Some burned through his clothes and penetrated his skin **"from the sole of his foot unto his crown"**.

Job's companions rushed him to shelter in the near-by cave. They lay the injured Job on the floor of the cave where he, in great pain from the multitude of burns, passes in and out of consciousness.

When Job is able to listen, one of Job's companions tries to say what has happened.

The fire of God is fallen from heaven, and hath burned up the sheep, and thy servants, and consumed them.... Job 1:16

And, behold, there came a great wind from the wilderness, and smote the four corners of the house, and it fell upon (thy sons and thy daughters) and they are dead.... Job 1:19

This is clearly a description of the events which describes the scientific evidence of this disaster. Rewrites and attempted clarifications down through the ages made by scribes, et al who did not witness the events, and who could not imagine such occurrences, have altered the original writing. But the basic story facts are left intact.

One of Job's "priestly" companions, Eliphaz tries to justify God's action in sending this disaster. In his attempt, he further describes the events.

By the blast of God they perish, and by the breath of his nostrils are they consumed. Job 4:9

Although affliction cometh not forth of the dust, neither doth trouble spring out of the ground; Job 5:6

Yet man is born unto trouble as the sparks fly upward. Job 5:7

"As the sparks fly upward" has been translated by scholars Maurer and Gesenius from the available Hebrew documents to say "As the sons of lighting fly high". That is, the disaster, the trouble, does not come from Earth, but from above; from the heavens.

Eliphaz continues in his attempts to convince Job that God has His own reasons for this disaster and that man should not question God.

I would seek unto God, and unto God would I commit my cause; Job 5:8

Which doeth great things, and unsearchable marvelous things without number. Job 5:9

Eliphaz gives examples of what God can do. He describes good things and bad things, such as this disaster.

They meet with darkness in the daytime, and grope in the noonday as in the night. Job 5:14

The sun has now been blotted out by the smoke and debris for a long time. And Eliphaz continues in his attempts to justify God's purposes and actions. But Job, in great pain from his burns, is not yet in the mood to hear someone try to justify God's actions. He believes he personally has done more good than bad.

Oh that my grief were thoroughly weighed, and my calamity laid in the balances together! Job 6:2

For the arrows of the Almighty are within me, the poison whereof drinkth up my spirit; the terrors of God do set themselves in array against me. Job 6:4

He is lamenting of his wounds, and the poisons festering in his burns. He prefers death to this suffering.

Oh that I might have my request; and that God would grant me the thing I long for! Job 6:8

Even that it would please God to destroy me; that he would let loose his hand and cut me off. Job 6:9

What is my strength that I should hope? And what is mine end, that I should prolong my life? Job 6:11

He points out what is happening to their people, as a result of the disaster. He speaks of ice in his semi-tropical country. And he speaks of the heat. Then he laments the faith of his people.

The paths of their way are turned aside; they go to nothing and perish. 6:18

And Job continues in his rebuff to his friend's words.

Teach me, and I will hold my tongue; and cause me to understand wherein I have erred. 6:24

Job turns sarcastic.

How forcible are right words! But what doth your arguing reprove? 6:25

He looks around him at the cave in which they have taken refuge.

Yea, ye overwhelm the fatherless, and, ye dig a pit for your friend. 6:27

Is there not an appointed time to man upon Earth? Are not his days also like the days of a hireling? 7:1

He wonders when the suffering will end.

When I lie down, I say, when shall I arise, and the night be gone? 7:4

He has been in the cave for a long time. The smoke and debris outside has blocked the sun's rays. There is no "day". He wonders when the Night will be gone.

He paints us a picture of his grave, pitiful position.

My flesh is clothed with worms and clods of dust; my skin is broken and become loathsome. 7:5

My days ... are spent without hope. 7:6

Job's anger shows.

Therefore I will not refrain my mouth; I will speak in the anguish of my spirit; I will complain in the bitterness of my soul. 7:11

He is miserable, disgusted. He believes he has been treated unfairly. He is angry. He wonders what he has done that was so bad as to deserve this. Why can't he be forgiven for whatever it was?

And why dost Thou not pardon my transgression and take away mine iniquity? For now shall I sleep in the dust; and Thou shall seek me in the morning, but I shall not be. 7:21

He truly feels helpless in his cave while the disaster continues outside. He believes he will die in the cave.

Job's companion, Bildad tries to affirm God's justice. Job answers with questions.

I know it is so of a truth; but how should man be just with God? 9:2

How can man be just with a God that does terrible things? He describes the terrible things of which God did.

Which removeth the mountains, and they know not; which overturneth them in his anger; 9:5

Which shaketh the Earth out of her place, and the pillars thereof tremble; 9:6

Which commandeth the sun, and it riseth not; and sealeth up the stars; 9:7

Which alone spreadeth out the heavens, and treadeth upon the waves of the sea. 9:8

Here Job has described the Earthquakes and volcanic actions, and the great pall of smoke and debris that blocks out the sun for a very long time, and the great waves of sea water that sweep the land.

And Job continues.

Behold, He taketh away, who can hinder Him? Who will say unto Him, what doest Thou? 9:12

That is, who can stop God? And who can question God?

If God will not withdraw His anger, the proud helpers do stoop under Him. 9:13

That is, if He will not withdraw his anger from the innocent and obedient:

How much less shall I answer Him, and choose out my words to reason with Him? 9:14

Job continues his questionings, and then describes the bad things God has done to him.

For He breaketh me with a tempest, and multiplied my wounds without cause. 9:17

He will not suffer me to take my breath, but filleth me with bitterness. 9:18

Job continues his questioning argument and draws some conclusions.

This is one thing, therefore I said it: He destroyed the perfect and the wicked. 9:22

He is accusing God of being angry and non-caring, of taking lives of everyone, even the perfect and innocent.

He believes God has given the Earth over to Satan.

If the scourge slay suddenly, he will laugh at the trial of the innocent. 9:23

The scourge is the body from heaven: Satan. Satan is causing the great disaster.

The Earth is given into the hand of the wicked... 9:24

That is, he believes God has given the Earth over to Satan. He asks: is this not so?

.... If not, where, and who is he? 9:24

Job now believes that his questioning and open statements against God will surely condemn him.

I know (now) that Thou wilt not hold me innocent. 9:26

And Job believes that no matter what he does, God will punish him.

Yet shall Thou plunge me in the ditch, and mine own clothes shall abhor me. 9:31

God has placed him in this ditch-like cave of filth. And there is no way for him to communicate effectively with God.

For He is not a man, as I am, that I should answer Him, and we should come together in judgment. 9:32

And Job continues to point out that there is also no one to act as a go-between. So Job despairs and then decides to plea for the mercy of God.

My soul is weary of my life; I will leave my complaint upon myself; I will speak in the bitterness of my soul. 10:1

I will say unto God, do not condemn me; show me wherefore Thou contendest with me. 10:2

He asks God to tell him what he has done? He continues in this vein, and then asks:

Are not my days few? Cease then, and let me alone, that I may take comfort a little. 10:20

Before I go whence I shall not return, even to (this) the land of darkness and the shadow of death. 10:21

A land of darkness, as darkness itself; and of the shadow of death, without any order, and where the light is as darkness. 10:22

Job argues that, since his remaining days are few, perhaps he should leave the cave and face the blackness of chaos outside the cave – and thus end his miserable life.

His companion, Zophas, is fearful for his soul and believes that he, Zophas, should chastise Job for such words.

And when thou mockest (God), shall no man make thee ashamed? 11:3

If He cut off, and shut up, or gather together, then who can hinder Him? 11:11

Zophas is telling Job that they cannot prevent God from doing God's will. But perhaps:

If thou prepare thine heart, and stretch out thine hands towards Him... 11:13

Then maybe it will soon all be over.

Because thou shalt forget thy misery, and remember it as waters that pass away. 11:16

And thine age shall be clearer than noonday; thou shalt shine forth, thou shalt be as the morning. 11:17

That is, it will be over, this age of darkness, and then morning will return.

And thou shalt be secure, because there is hope; yea, thou shalt dig about thee, and thou shalt take rest in safety. 11:18

That is, the great tempest will pass. The waters will pass away and then we will dig ourselves out of this cave and find a safe place for rest.

It is obvious that Job's companions include the holy men of his time. That is why they keep defending God against Job's remarks.

The Holy men of that time were also the keepers of the great knowledge of the civilization and religion, and this positions Job's response.

No doubt but ye are the people, and wisdom shall die with you. 12:2

But I have understanding as well as you; I am not inferior to you; yea, who knoweth not such things as these. 12:3

So Job scolds the "Priests" for chastising him.

It should perhaps be noted at this point just who Job and his companions were.

The Arabians declare that Job's father was the founder of the Arabian peoples. Job then, was most likely the son of the King. That is perhaps why he was rescued and taken to the cave; and why "priests" were with him.

It also helps explain Job's stance, his comments and arguments, and the pro-god arguments of his companions.

Job continues his arguments, noting that the priests, these wise men, his companions, "pretend" that God has only destroyed and made the wicked suffer. He argues if they believe that the sins of men have brought this disaster, go ask the innocent beasts and birds.

But ask now the beasts, and they shall teach thee; and the fowls of the air, and they shall tell thee. 12:7

Or speak to the Earth and it shall teach thee; and the fishes of the sea shall declare unto thee. 12:8

They have almost all been destroyed.

Job continues in this vein, and then acknowledges the ancient knowledge of the priests.

With the ancient is wisdom; and in length of days understandings. 12:12

This "length of days" refers to the knowledge of the movements of the Gods (planets and stars).

But look what God is doing now.

Behold, He breaketh down, and it cannot be built again; He shutteth up a man, and there can be no opening. 12:14

Behold, He withholdeth the waters and they dry up. Also He sendeth them out, and they overturn the Earth. 12:15

This summarizes some of the events previously described.

He discovereth deep things out of the darkness, and bringeth out to light the shadow of death. 12:22

That is, God brought something out of the darkness of the heavens, and these "deep things" brought death.

The priests call it Satan.

He taketh away the heart of the Chief of the people of the Earth and causeth them to wander in a wilderness where there is no way. 12:24

He may be referring here to the death of his father the King. In any event, he is referring to the death of their leader.

They grope in the dark without light, and He maketh them to stagger like a drunken man. 12:25

Job speaks of the people that have left their shelters after the great waves have swept across the land. Job probably also looked outside the cave but was too weak to go out with any of them. It is also likely that some of the people that went outside returned to report to Job and the priests.

Lo, mine eye hath seen all this, mine ear have heard and understood it. 13:1

What ye know, the same do I know also. I am not inferior unto you. 13:3

Job obviously resents the priests "talking down to him".

Surely I would speak to the Almighty, and I desire to reason with God. 13:3

Job wants to talk with, and reason with God, as opposed to the priests' position of simple faith in God doing His will.

But ye are forgers of lies; ye are all physicians of no value. 13:4

Oh that ye would altogether hold your peace! 13:5

Job, who has probably been taught to respect the priests' wisdom in religious matters, no longer sees reason for such respect. He, in effect, tells them to shut up!

Hold your peace, let me alone, that I may speak, and let come on me what will. 13:13

Job wants the priests to stop justifying God's terrible actions and to stop trying to stifle him in fear that God will destroy his soul.

.... If I hold my tongue, I shall give up the ghost. 13:19

But man dieth, and wasteth away. Yea, man giveth up the ghost, and where is he? 14:10

Then Job asks for God's mercy.

Oh that Thou wouldest hide me in the grave, that Thou wouldest keep me a secret, until Thy wrath be past. 14:13

Job asks God to let him die – to then forget him until His anger has passed and He is ready to let Job live again.

If a man die, shall he live again? 14:14

Job tells God he will be ready when He calls for him. Then he provides more insight into the disaster, which, for brevity, is not repeated here.

Then Eliphaz again rebuffs Job.

Should a wise man utter vain knowledge, and fill his belly with east wind (nonsense). 15:2

Should he reason with unprofitable talk? Or with speeches wherewith he can do no good? 15:3

And Eliphaz continues to scold Job. And Job answers.

I have (now) heard many such things. Miserable comforters are ye all! 16:2

Job basically dismisses all their comments and arguments. Then Job discusses – in an analogist manner – what bad things God is doing to him, and concludes:

God hath delivered me to the ungodly, and has turned me over into the hands of the wicked. 16:11.

Satan.

Job continues to bemoan what God had done to him, and then resigns himself with:

My friends scorn me. 16:20

At this point it appears that Job breaks down, crying.

My friends scorn me: but mine eye poureth out tears unto God. 16:20

And then Job rambles on, continuing to complain. Then, in a manner of speech, he tried to make amends with God.

And where is now my hope? As for my hope, who shall see it? 17:15

They shall go down to the bars of the pit, when our rest together is in the dust. 17:16

Job believes there is no hope – and no one to know of hope – and at best, they'll be found in the cave long after they are dead.

Bildad has heard enough. He interrupts.

How long will it be ere ye make an end of words? 18:2

That is, when will you shut up?

Then Bildad goes into another religious speech, describing the fate of the wicked.

Then Job tires of Bildad's speech.

How long will ye vex my soul, and break me in pieces with words? 19:2

Job gives another speech and then speaks of his condition.

My bone cleaveth to my skin and to my flesh, and I am escaped with the skin of my teeth. 19:20

Have pity upon me, have pity upon me, o ye my friends, for the hand of God hath touched me. 19:21

They are starving; just skin and bones. Job asks his companions to go easy on him; he is the one with the festering wounds.

Then he makes three very important statements.

```
¶
Oh·that·my·words·were·
written!··Oh·that·they·were·
printed·in·a·book!·19:23¶
¶
For·I·know·that·my·Redeemer·
liveth,·and·that·he·shall·stand·
at·the·latter·day·upon·the·
earth.·19:25¶
¶
And·though·after·my·skin·
worms·destroy·this·body,·yet·
in·my·flesh·shall·I·see·God.·
19:26¶
¤
```

Job acknowledges God and wants the discussion here in the cave, including details of the disaster, to be written down. This desire on his part is probably why we have this extraordinary account of the disaster.

Their discussions and arguments continue. Eliphaz tries to convince Job that he has not been that good to his people.

Thou hast not given water to the weary to drink, and thou hast withholden bread from the hungry. 22:7

That is, Job, as a rich man did not do all he could have done for the poor.

And besides, God may not know what is going on now, i.e. how bad it is now:

Is not God in the height of heaven? And behold the height of the stars, how high they are! 22:12

Can He judge through the dark cloud? 22:13

Thick clouds are a covering to Him, that He seeth not. 22:14

Job then responds and complains of God's indifference to wickedness. He observes that God seems to treat the good and bad equally.

Bildad then denies that man can be justified with God.

And Job agues back. A section of Job's arguments are particularly informative re the disaster.

Hell is naked before Him, and destruction hath no covering. 26:6

God has released hell on Earth.

He stretcheth out the north over the empty place, and hangeth the Earth upon nothing. 26:7

The chunk came from the north, and now Earth has been set loose from its position in the heavens, and among the sun, moon, and stars.

He bindeth up the waters in his thick clouds; and the cloud is not rent under them. 26:8

Here he describes his version of the events described in the scientific section where much of Earth's water is evaporated up into heavy dense clouds, but the waters are not released as rain. It may be recalled from that section that there was still too much heat for the clouds to condense and fall as rain. The rains occurred later when the Earth cooled and the clouds could condense as previously described.

He holdeth back the face of his throne, and spreadeth his cloud upon it 26:9

He has compassed the waters with bounds, until the day and night come to an end. 26:10

117

The clouds cover the sun and heaven, and there is no night or day –
just darkness.

**The pillars of heaven tremble, and are astonished at his
reproof. 26:11**

**He divideth the sea with his power, and by His
understanding He smiteth through the proud. 26:12**

**By His Spirit He hath garnished the heavens; his hand
hath formed the crooked serpent. 26:13**

He caused Earthquakes and Earth crust shifts and volcanic
eruptions. He caused the sea to "pile up" and much of it to
evaporate. He killed almost all life. He smashed Tiamat and
spread bodies of fire across the heavens – before the clouds
formed. And most importantly, He formed the swarm of matter
that rushed Earth in its undulating path as previously described.

This undulating "crooked serpent" was Satan.

Job rambles on and talks of the wicked. Did they cause this? And
he speaks of man's quest for understanding; and he recalls his
former glory as the King's son.

**Oh that I were as in months past, as in the days when God
preserved me. 29:2**

When His candle shined upon my head. 29:3

**The young men saw me, and hid themselves; and the aged
arose, and stood up. 29:8**

And he continues, describing his position, his power, and the good
deeds he did for his people. And then he speaks of the present
condition of his people.

**For want and famine they were solitary, fleeing into the
wilderness in former time desolate and waste. 30:3**

**Who cut up mallows by the bushes, and juniper roots for
their meat. 30:4**

They were driven forth from among men... 30:5

To dwell in the cliffs of the valleys, in the caves of the Earth, and in the rocks. 30:6

During the early part of the disaster, solitary individuals, and small groups such as Job and his companions, ran for the cliffs, rocks, and caves to escape death. Those that didn't were destroyed. The only food they could find in the early darkness was roots and scattered plant parts. They probably also found some dead animals parts.

Job talks of his loss of leadership. He laments of his inability to help his people and his now low position. And then:

.... The days of affliction have taken hold upon me. 30:16

He have cast me into the mire, and I am become like dust and ashes. 30:19

God has sent the fire that burned his body, and forced him into this filthy cave.

I cry unto Thee, and Thou dost not hear me. I stand up and Thou regardest me not. 30:20

Thou art become cruel to me. 30:21

And Job cannot understand why God is being so cruel to him. Job believes he has only done well.

Was not my soul grieved for the poor? 30:25

But look what God has done to me.

When I looked for good, then evil came upon me. And when I waited for light, there came darkness. 30:26

Job just cannot understand why this is all happening. He continues his questioning and arguments.

He is then followed by the younger Elihu who makes the following points.

I am young, and ye are very old; wherefore I… durst not show you mine opinion. 32:6

But now:

I will answer… (And) show mine opinion. 32:17

Wherefore, Job, I pray thee, hear my speeches. 33:1

…. God is greater than man. 33:12

Why dost thou strive against Him? For He giveth not account of any of His matters. 33:13

And Elihyu thus reproves Job and justifies God, and extols God's greatness.

The entire style of writing then changes with God speaking directly to Job. It seems clear, as many Biblical scholars agree, that this latter part of the Book of Job was rewritten in much more recent times.

It still contains phrases relating to the disaster and its aftermath – but apparently the latter writer did not understand the context, and the resulting rewrite appears to be an attempt to "resolve the conflict", as is the traditional custom for writing the end of fictional stories, which the latter writer apparently believed the original to be.

Some examples of God speaking to Job, making the point that God is greater than Job, are obviously rewrites of the disaster in that they contain key elements of the disaster.

Where wast thou when I laid the foundations of the Earth? 38:4

Do you know?

Where is the way where light dwelleth? 38:19

Hast thou entered into the treasures of the snow? Or hast thou seen the treasures of the hail? 38:22

Hath the rain a father? Or who hath begotten the drops of dew? 38:28

And God refers to the disaster:

Out of whose womb came the ice? And the hoary frost of heaven, who hath gendered it? 38:29

Here the new writer has God show Job His greatness and uniqueness by asking these questions – but note that the questions retain their context of the disaster: snow, hail, ice, hoary frost, etc. This seems to refer to the great cold that followed the disaster.

It appears that Job and his companions continued to write about this phase of the aftermath, and it got edited and rewritten in this manner with God speaking directly to Job.

And then the new writer has Job respond to God's statements.

I know that Thou canst do everything. 42:2

Therefore have I uttered that which I understood not. 42:3

But now I seeth, I understand, and...

.... Wherefore I abhor myself, and repent in dust and ashes. 42:6

And so God forgives job and orders his companions to make animal sacrifices for Job. God restores Job's prosperity and:

.... Lived Job a hundred and 40 years... 42:16

So it is quite clear that later scribes, et al did not understand this very ancient document. But in spite of their lack of understanding and mistranslations, we can clearly see that the Book of Job is an eyewitness account of the events of the great disaster previously described in scientific terms.

We will never know what truly happened to Job because later editors gave a happy, if almost impossible, ending to Job's story.

I believe that John had the original or at least an early version of the document of Job's ordeal in the cave. I believe that he and other writers of parts of the Bible realized that this was a sacred document and they passed along its messages in their writings.

It is noted, however that they wrote many centuries later and could not truly comprehend the amazing event. They tried to "improve" it to make it more understandable and in so doing may have changed some of the basic story.

But we still have the voice of Job, bold, defiant, unshrinking, protesting the cruelty of nature, of God, and appealing from God's awful deed to the sense of justice.

We have mankind's oldest, surviving written document; a ringside seat to, arguable, the greatest event in man's history!

Chapter 7
The Mountain Cave

Their ruler, riding on a storm…. Stepped down from heaven to the great Earth. **Lugalbanda of Sumer: In the Mountain Cave**

It is interesting to note that a somewhat similar story to that of Job was found in Sumerian clay tablets. These tablets were written and most likely edited and copied from more ancient documents over 4000 years ago.

It may be that both Job and the Sumerian story were derived from an original document written even earlier.

The Sumerian story could, of course, be about a different person that also hid in a mountain cave to escape the disaster. See which you think is the case.

Only brief excerpts are presented here.

The ruling god, Enlil, son of Utu (the sun), **"riding on a storm…. Stepped down from heaven to the great Earth. His head shines with brilliance, the barbed arrows flash past him like lightning…."**

This sounds like the chunk of material the Hebrews called Satan.

In the great mountains, a sickness befell Lugalbanda. His brother and friends try to make him comfortable in a cave. Later, believing Lugalbanda will die, they leave him in the mountain cave.

Sounds like Lugalbanda's companions finally escaped the cave and left him there to die.

Later the sun shines through the clouds and Lugalbanda awakens.

When he lifted his eyes to heaven to Utu (the sun), he wept to him as if to his own father. In the mountain cave he raised to him his fair hands:

Lugalbanda

"Utu, I greet you! Let me be ill no longer!

Don't make me eat saltpeter as if it were barley!

Don't make me fall like a throw stick somewhere in the desert unknown to me!

Let me not come to an end in the mountains like a weakling!"

Utu accepted his tears. He sent down his divine encouragement to him in the mountain cave.

And all ended well.

This seems very similar to the events described in the Book of Job.

Chapter 8
When Where Why

"I could prove God statistically." **George Gallup**

Did God inspire John to write Revelation or did John just copy parts of old scrolls and piece Revelation together?

Maybe God inspired him by giving him the old scrolls.

In any event, considering the limited knowledge about asteroids during John's times, John got a fairly good description of what happened to Job and others many centuries earlier.

When we combine Revelation and all of the other ancient writings with our new knowledge of what happened scientifically, we can clearly understand John's forecast of our end.

An asteroid or similar heavenly body will eventually destroy us.

The only remaining questions are when and can we do anything to delay the inevitability.

Let's try to better understand the When-Where-Why of the impact in Revelation to help us get answers.

When

The disaster happened about 11,632 years ago; 9619 BC.

The carbon dated deposits of plant and animal materials that coincide with the same dates for major worldwide geological changes clearly prove that there was a worldwide disaster that struck Earth in about 9619 BC.

Carbon dating masses of plant materials buried by the disaster yields an average date of 11, 527 years ago. Similar dating of buried animal deposits yields an average date of 11,680 years ago for the "old world" and 11,574 for the "new world", principally the United States and Canada.

Two separate dating of displaced and buried sea shells indicate average dates of 11,543 and 11,552 years ago.

Major geological displacements have been dated in the old world as occurring at an average of 11,592 years ago.

Converting these data gives a range for the occurrence from 9516 BC to 9669 BC.

Simply averaging all of these dates yields an average of 9559 BC. Providing some weighting since the various numbers varied a bit, yields a most likely time of 9619 BC.

The time of year can be determined more precisely. There were large numbers of newborn animals buried in the disaster, which indicated spring or early summer.

Plant remains found in the stomachs of the Siberian mammoths frozen in the disaster and in the plant materials buried in the disaster, show that early summer was the season of the disaster.

In the ancient Persian story of the disaster, it is recorded that the disaster occurred in the zodiacal constellation of Cancer. This would have been the month of April.

Therefore **April of 9619 BC** was selected as the most likely date for the disaster.

Where

The disaster covered the entire Earth, except for some of the highest mountains.

Satan's path was from the northwest to the southeast.

Arctic Region

Fossil evidence in the Arctic regions show convincing evidence of great changes in land elevations: some land submerged and some rose significantly in elevation.

The existing drainage systems were almost all completely changed at that time.

There were large lateral crystal displacements, crystal tilting, and over thrusting of older over younger strata.

Some of the major fissures and fractures that occurred still exist.

The Americas

Most of the Americas greatly increased in elevation. However Florida, the east coast, Honduras and some of the Caribbean area subsided.

There was great volcanic activity in most of the Americas.

There was a significant sinking of the Appalachia Mountains.

Atlantic

Similar events occurred in the North Atlantic Region. Some of the lands of Greenland also sank.

Land around the Azores sank beneath the ocean.

Plato records that this was the sinking of Atlantis. Significant volcanism occurred in the Azores.

Europe

Similar events also occurred in most of Europe. Most of Europe experienced significant changes in elevations. Great fissures and fractures opened in the British Isles, Irish Sea, the North Sea, and in Norway and the Ural Mountains.

Asia

Most of the mountains of Asia increased in elevation, however some areas sank.

Africa

Much of Africa increased in elevation. Lake levels and the basic drainage system was changed.

Pacific Region

Most of the areas in the Pacific Region, except for the Mindanao Islands, sank. The Mindanao Islands increased in elevation.

Australia and Oceania

Some of Indonesia and much of the area increased in elevation while much of Indonesia, the Indian Ocean, and some of the other areas sank.

Most of the area experienced increased volcanism. Many land bridges and landmasses disappeared completely.

Summary

Analyses of the debris deposits and their locations allow us to calculate the trajectory of the "intruder" and the explosion of one of the large bodies orbiting about the intruder; i.e. Tiamat's moon Kingu.

From these analyses it is clear that the great disaster and the following flood occurred over all of the Earth, just as stated in the Bible:

And the waters prevailed exceedingly upon the Earth; and all the high hills, that were under the whole haven, were covered. Genesis 7:19

The great disaster destroyed almost all life on Earth. Many complete species such as the Wooly Mammoth and Saber-Tooth Tiger became extinct.

The entire Earth and all its life forms were forever changed by the event.

The heavy debris and water-laden clouds completely blocked out the sun for at least 3 years. There was almost total darkness.

Eventually scattered sunrays began to break through the thinning clouds, but it was decades before anything like a full day-night cycle returned to Earth.

We now well know the When and Where of the great disaster because it was so very well recorded in the debris fields, great terrestrial scars and geological changes that it left us.

And the memory of the great disaster has been well recorded in the folklore, legends, "myths", and written records, some of which have been presented herein.

We very well know that the great disaster really did happen. And we well know when and where it happened.

It occurred all over the Earth beginning in about April 9619 BC.

When the ancient societies recorded this great disaster, they not only left us with the When and Where information, they also gave us their version of why as previously presented.

Why

The destruction was caused by a chunk of material from outer space.

To better understand Why, let's review the ancient documentation.

The oldest record of the disaster, written long before the beginning of the Hebrews and their religion, was later modified and incorporated in the Hebrew Bible as the Book of Job.

In the Book of Job, God brags of Job's loyalty and Satan responds:

But put forth thine hand now, and touch all that he hath, and he will curse thee to thy face. Job 1:11

And the Lord said unto Satan, Behold, all that he (Job) hath is in thy power.... Genesis 1:12

So, according to this oldest written account, Satan causes the great disaster to tempt Job to curse God.

Genesis, however, tells us that:

And God said unto Noah, the end of all flesh is come before me; for the Earth is filled with violence through them; and, behold, I will destroy them with the Earth. Genesis 6:13

And, behold, I, even I, do bring a flood of waters upon the Earth, to destroy all flesh, wherein is the breath of life, from under heaven; and every thing that is in the Earth shall die. Genesis 6:17

So it appears that the Bible gives us two different reasons for sending the disaster:

To tempt Job

To destroy mankind

I believe, along with major scholars Magee, Schultens, Lowth, and Michaelis that the first parts of the Book of Job were added many

131

centuries after the basic body of the Book had been written. The new writer had not witnessed the disaster as Job had, and did not understand the true context of the Book.

The new writers wrote this front part in an effort to give a reason for the terrible trials to which Job had been subjected. They did not understand the scientific facts that caused the disaster.

If this position is accepted, then we have the Bible telling us:

And God saw that the wickedness of man was great in the Earth, and that every imagination of the thoughts of his heart was only evil continually. Genesis 6:5

And the Lord said I will destroy man whom I have created from the face of the Earth.... Genesis 6:7

Now, going back to the second oldest written document, the clay tablets of ancient Sumer, we learn that Gilgamesh, the King of ancient Uruk, goes on a mission to seek Utnapishtim, the Sumerian Noah, whom the gods have made immortal after the flood ordeal.

Utnapishtim tells Gilgamesh why the flood came about:

King of Uruk, surely there is no one more bold.

Here is knowledge that no other has ever been told.

Near where Euphrates born sits a city you call Shuruppak, home of those divine.

Enlil sent from there a flood to stop noisy human babbling all the time.

So the ancient clay tablets of Sumer tell us that the god Enlil caused the flood to stop human noise!

The ancient documents tell us different reasons for the disaster:

To tempt Job;

The wickedness of mankind;

Mankind making too much noise;

A god drove the sun too close to Earth.

All of the ancient documentations, however, tell us that God, or a god, caused the disaster.

There are several different documented versions of these Biblical and Sumerian reasons for the flood, but all basically say that the gods caused the disaster for one of these two reasons.

There are also many other versions, most of which describe the event, but do not give a reason. Many of these were documented centuries later and may therefore be less accurate.

Perhaps the best example of these later, **imaged versions** is that documented by Ovid where Phaeton, the son of the god Apollo, drives the chariot of the sun too close to Earth and sets the world on fire.

From the scientific evidence, we know that the disaster was caused by a chunk of material from outer space that has been called a lot of different names.

I guess the name Satan is as good as any.

It is clear why the writers did not understand the Why of the disaster. How could they? No one at that time understood asteroids.

They just could not understand that something falling from the sky could do such damage.

But we now know the Why: materials from the Vela Supernova rained down on planet Earth.

But with or without understanding the Why, many writers recorded what **did happen** on Earth. They recorded what they saw in the terms of their understandings at the time.

John understood that the event really happened and he believed, either divinely or through logic, that it would happen again.

John has foretold that an asteroid will be the end of us.

Chapter 9
Asteroids, Comets and Meteorite Impacts

Nothing in life is to be feared, it is only to be understood. Now is the time to understand more, so that we may fear less. **Marie Curie**

I believe that Revelation is correct in foretelling that an asteroid will be the end of us.

We need to better understand asteroids and see if we can use technology to delay our destruction as long as possible.

Probably the best known impacts on Earth are the asteroid that destroyed the dinosaurs about 65 million years and the impact in Arizona about 50 thousands years ago that is still very visible.

Crater in Arizona

But there have been many, many more.

The more recent impacts in Russia in 1908 and in 2013 are making all of us realize that impacts of asteroids and comets are major threats to our existence.

These impacts are making us much more interested in just what Revelation has told us.

Let's try to access just how high our risks really are; and maybe get an idea of the timing for our end.

And on a more optimistic note; maybe learn how to delay the inevitability.

Let's start by understanding the names of the heavenly objects that impact Earth.

Asteroids are generally rocky and larger than meteoroids, but smaller than planets.

Comets contain frozen liquids or gases that evaporate and create a luminous tail as the objects approach the sun.

A meteor or shooting star is the visible streak of light that occurs when a meteoroid enters the Earth's atmosphere.

The portion of a meteor that survives the passage through the atmosphere and reaches the ground is called a meteorite.

Our primary discussions will generally be limited to deadly asteroids and comets and for simplicity, we will refer to both as asteroids since comets and asteroids cause similar results when they hit Earth.

It has been estimated based on a computer simulation that during the last 10,000 years we have been hit about 350 times by asteroids as large as the rock that wasted 2,000 square kilometers of Siberian forest in 1908.

Asteroids that could cause a global catastrophe, such as one that kills more than one-quarter of humanity, has been estimated to occur about every 330,000 years.

Let's review a little more of the data for each type of potential impact.

Asteroids

Asteroids range in size from tiny grains to "minor planets". The larger ones are sometimes called planetoids. However the term asteroid is increasingly used specifically to the small bodies of the inner Solar System out to the orbit of Jupiter.

There are millions of asteroids and they are generally thought to be the shattered remnants of bodies within the young Sun's solar nebula that never grew large enough to become planets.

The large majority of known asteroids orbit in the asteroid belt between the orbits of Mars and Jupiter or co-orbit with Jupiter. However, other orbital families exist with significant populations, including the near-Earth asteroids.

These are objects in a near-Earth orbit without the tail or coma of a comet. As of May 2012, 8,880 near-Earth asteroids are known and range in size from 1 meter up to about 32 kilometers. The number of near-Earth asteroids over one kilometer in diameter is estimated to be about 981.

Some asteroids are large enough to have their own "moons" as does 243 Ida as shown here.

243 Ida with its Moon Dactyl

The tiny dot to the right is its moon, Dactyl.

Ida is irregularly shaped with an average diameter of 31.4 kilometers. Its surface has a wide variety of crater sizes and ages, and is one of the most heavily cratered in the Solar System.

Ida's moon, Dactyl is only 1.4 kilometers in diameter, about one-twentieth the size of Ida.

Comets

A comet is a small icy Solar System body that, when close enough to the Sun, displays a visible coma typically called a tail. This tail is due to the effects of solar radiation and the solar wind that causes the comet to "out gas" and glow.

Comet nuclei range from a few hundred meters to tens of kilometers across and are composed of loose collections of ice, dust, and small rocky particles.

Comets have been observed since ancient times.

Comets have a wide range of orbital periods ranging from a few years to hundreds of thousands of years. Short-period comets originate in the Kuiper belt which lies beyond the orbit of Neptune.

Longer-period comets are thought to originate in the Oort cloud which is a hypothesized spherical cloud of icy bodies in the outer Solar System. Long-period comets plunge towards the Sun from the Oort cloud because of gravitational perturbations caused by either the massive outer planets of the Solar System (Jupiter, Saturn, Uranus, and Neptune), or by passing stars.

Comets are distinguished from asteroids by the presence of a coma or a tail. However, extinct comets that have passed close to the Sun many times have lost nearly all of their volatile ices and dust and may come to resemble small asteroids.

As of January 2011 there were a reported 4,185 known comets of which about 1,500 are a family of "sun-grazing" comets that are characterized by orbits that take them extremely close to the Sun. They are believed to be fragments of one large comet that broke up several centuries ago.

There are also about 484 short-period comets and their numbers are steadily increasing.

These two set of comets represents only a tiny fraction of the total comet population. It is believed that comet-like bodies in the outer Solar System may number over one trillion.

Halley's Comet

Halley's Comet is perhaps the best known comet. It is visible with the naked eye every 75-76 years.

Other naked-eye comets may be brighter and more spectacular, but will appear only once in thousands of years.

Halley's Comet has been observed and recorded as long ago as at least 240 BC. Clear records of the comet's appearances were made by Chinese, Babylonians, and Medieval Europeans. However the appearances were not recognized as reappearances of the same object at those early times. The comet's periodicity was first determined in 1705 by English astronomer Edmond Halley, after whom it is now named.

Halley's Comet last appeared in the inner Solar System in 1986 and will next appear in mid-2061.

Meteor Shower

As a result of out gassing, comets leave a trail of solid debris. If the comet's path crosses Earth's path, then at that point there are likely to be meteor showers as Earth passes through the trail of debris.

The Perseid meteor shower, for example, occurs every year between August 9 and August 13, when Earth passes through the orbit of Comet Swift-Tuttle.

Halley's Comet is the source of the Orionid shower in October.

Comet Shoemaker-Levy

Comet Shoemaker-Levy broke apart as it approached Jupiter. Its impact on Jupiter left several brown spots as depicted.

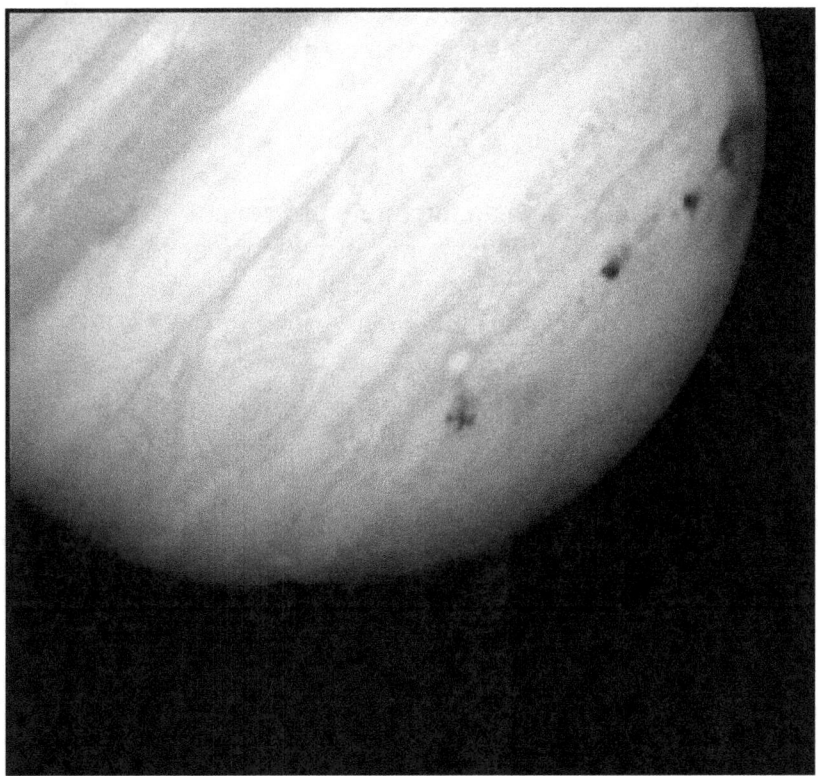

Early Comets

Collisions between comets and planets or moons were common in the early Solar System: some of the many craters on the Earth's Moon were caused by comets.

Many comets and asteroids collided into Earth in its early stages. Many scientists believe that comets bombarding the young Earth (about 4 billion years ago) brought the vast quantities of water that now fill the Earth's oceans, or at least a significant portion of it.

The detection of organic molecules in comets has led some to speculate that comets or meteorites may have brought the precursors of life, or even life itself, to Earth. You can learn more about this from my book: **Life and the Universe** at http://www.amazon.com/dp/B00BYJISQE

There are still many near-Earth comets, although a collision with an asteroid is more likely than with a comet.

Before the invention of the telescope, comets seemed to appear out of nowhere in the sky and gradually vanish out of sight. They were usually considered bad omens of deaths of kings or noble men, or coming catastrophes, or even interpreted as attacks by heavenly beings against terrestrial inhabitants. From ancient sources, such as Chinese oracle bones, it is known that their appearances have been noticed by humans for millennia.

Some authorities interpret references to "falling stars" in the Babylonian Epic of Gilgamesh, in the Book of Revelation, and the Book of Enoch, all previously described, as references to comets and asteroids.

Recent Scientific Analyses of Comets

In July 2005, the Deep Impact probe, shown below in an artist's conception, blasted a crater on Comet Tempel 1 to study its interior.

The mission yielded results suggesting that the majority of a comet's water ice is below the surface, and that these reservoirs feed the jets of vaporized water that form the coma of Tempel 1.

The Stardust spacecraft, launched in February 1999, collected particles from the coma of Comet Wild 2 in January 2004, and returned the samples to Earth in a capsule in January 2006.

Claudia Alexander, a program scientist for Rosetta from NASA's Jet Propulsion Laboratory who has modeled comets for years, reported to space.com about her astonishment at the number of jets, their appearance on the dark side of the comet as well as on the light side, their ability to lift large chunks of rock from the surface of the comet and the fact that comet Wild 2 is not a loosely cemented rubble pile.

More recent data from the Stardust mission show that materials retrieved from the tail of Wild 2 were crystalline and could only have been "born in fire". Although comets formed in the outer Solar System, radial mixing of material during the early formation of the Solar System is thought to have redistributed material throughout the proto-planetary disk, so comets also contain crystalline grains that formed in the hot inner Solar System. This is seen in comet spectra as well as in samples from return missions.

More recent still, the materials retrieved demonstrate that the "comet dust resembles asteroid materials". These new results have forced scientists to rethink the nature of comets and their distinction from asteroids.

NASA is developing a comet harpoon for returning samples to Earth.

In April 2011, scientists from the University of Arizona discovered evidence for the presence of liquid water in a Comet Wild 2. They have found iron and copper sulfide minerals that must have formed in the presence of water. The discovery shatters the existing paradigm that comets never get warm enough to melt their icy bulk.

Forthcoming space missions will add greater detail to our understanding of what comets are made of.

Frequency of Comet Appearances

Comets visible to the naked eye are fairly infrequent, but comets that put on fine displays in amateur class telescopes (50 mm to 100 cm) occur fairly often, as often as several times a year, occasionally with more than one in the sky at the same time.

Meteoroids

A meteoroid is a celestial body composed of rock or metal ranging in size from a dust grain to about 10 meters in diameter. It is typically a small particle from a comet or asteroid.

In 1961, the International Astronomical Union defined a meteoroid as "a solid object moving in interplanetary space, of a size considerably smaller than an asteroid and considerably larger than an atom".

The composition of meteoroids can be inferred as they pass through Earth's atmosphere from their trajectories and the light spectra of the resulting meteor. From these trajectory measurements, meteoroids have been found to have many different orbits, some clustering in streams, called Meteor showers and some apparently sporadic.

Meteoroids travel around the Sun in a variety of orbits and at various velocities. The fastest ones move at about 42 kilometers per second through space in the vicinity of Earth's orbit. The Earth travels at about 29.6 kilometers per second. Thus, when meteoroids meet Earth's atmosphere head-on speed may reach about 71 kilometers per second. Meteoroids moving through Earth's orbital space average about 20 kilometers per second.

On January 17 of 2013 a one meter-sized comet from the Oort cloud entered Earth atmosphere and collided head-on with Earth atmosphere at about 72 kilometers per second and it vaporized over a period of several seconds at more than 100 kilometers above ground.

The visible streak of light from such space debris is the result of heat as it enters the planet's atmosphere, and the glowing particles that it sheds in its wake is called a meteor, or colloquially a "shooting star" or "falling star". Many meteors appearing seconds or minutes apart, and appearing to originate from the same fixed point in the sky, are called a meteor shower.

Objects larger than several meters can explode in the air and create damage.

Meteorites

If a meteoroid, comet or asteroid withstands ablation from its atmospheric entry and impacts with the ground, then it is called a meteorite.

Around 15,000 tons of meteoroids, micrometeoroids and different forms of space dust enter Earth's atmosphere each year.

A meteor or "shooting star" is the visible streak of light from a meteoroid or micrometeoroid, heated and glowing from entering the Earth's atmosphere, as it sheds glowing material in its wake. Millions of meteors occur in the Earth's atmosphere daily.

Most meteoroids that cause meteors are about the size of a pebble. Meteors may occur in showers, which arise when the Earth passes through a stream of debris left by a comet, or as "random" or "sporadic" meteors, not associated with a specific stream of space debris.

A number of specific meteors have been observed, mostly by accident by members of the public. The tremendous amount of detail data that has been collected has allowed the orbits to be calculated.

All of the orbits passed through the asteroid belt.

The visible light produced by a meteor may take on various hues, depending on the chemical composition of the meteoroid, and the speed of its movement through the atmosphere. As layers of the meteoroid abrade and ionize, the color of the light emitted may change according to the layering of minerals. Possible colors (and elements producing them) include:

Orange/yellow (sodium)
Yellow (iron)
Blue/green (copper)
Purple (potassium)
Red (silicate)

Entry of meteoroids into the Earth's atmosphere produces three main effects: ionization of atmospheric molecules, dust that the meteoroid sheds, and the sound of passage.

Some meteors may produce a sonic boom as they streak through the atmosphere.

Peekskill Meteorite

Perhaps the best-known meteor/meteorite fall is the Peekskill meteorite.

Peekskill
Stone, chondrite (ordinary, H)
Fell 1992
Westchester County, New York

The Peekskill meteorite is among the most historic meteorite events on record. Sixteen separate video recordings document the meteorite burning through the Earth's atmosphere and striking a parked car in Peekskill, New York.

The Peekskill meteorite is of the stony variety and approximately 20% of its mass is tiny flakes of nickel-iron. When it struck Earth it weighed 26 pounds (12 kilograms) and measured one foot in diameter. The Peekskill meteorite is estimated to be 4.4 billion years old.

Car Hit by Peekskill Meteorite

After it smashed through the trunk of her Chevy Malibu, 18-year old Michelle Knapp retrieved the meteorite, after which it was sold to a consortium of three dealers for more than $69,000. Small specimens of Peekskill now sell for approximately $125 per gram.

The car, as well as the main mass of the meteorite (which weighs 890 grams), are currently in the Macovich Collection of Meteorites.

Chapter 10
Dinosaur Killing Asteroid of 65 Million Years Ago

The dinosaurs became extinct because they didn't have a space program. And if we become extinct because we don't have a space program, it'll serve us right! **Larry Niven**

A great deal of study and analyses have resulted in us having a fairly good understanding of the asteroid impact that destroyed the dinosaurs. It was a 10-kilometer asteroid or comet that struck just north of the Yucatan Peninsula 65 million years ago. It was traveling 30 kilometers per second, 150 times faster than a jet airliner.

It caused a global firestorm followed by a cold snap and finally a global warming all working together that extinguished the dinosaurs.

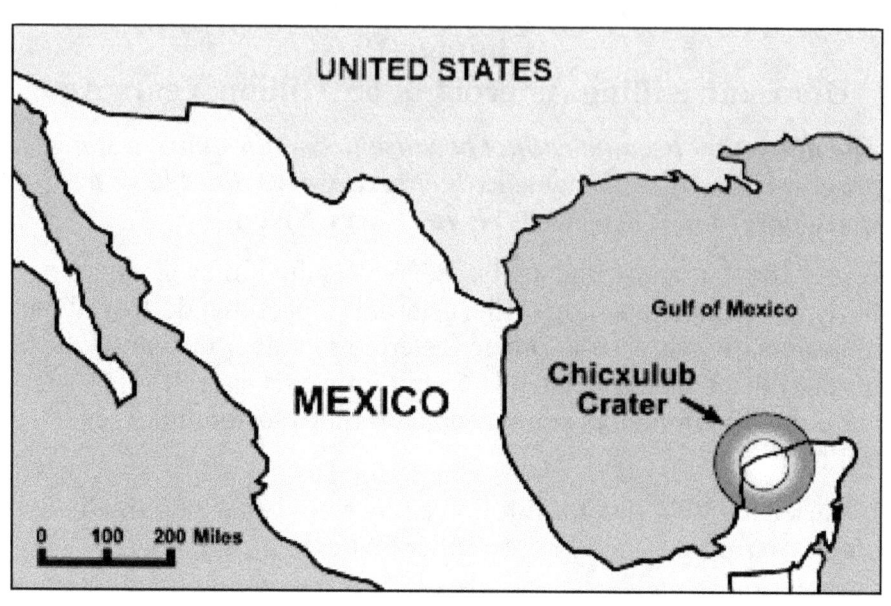

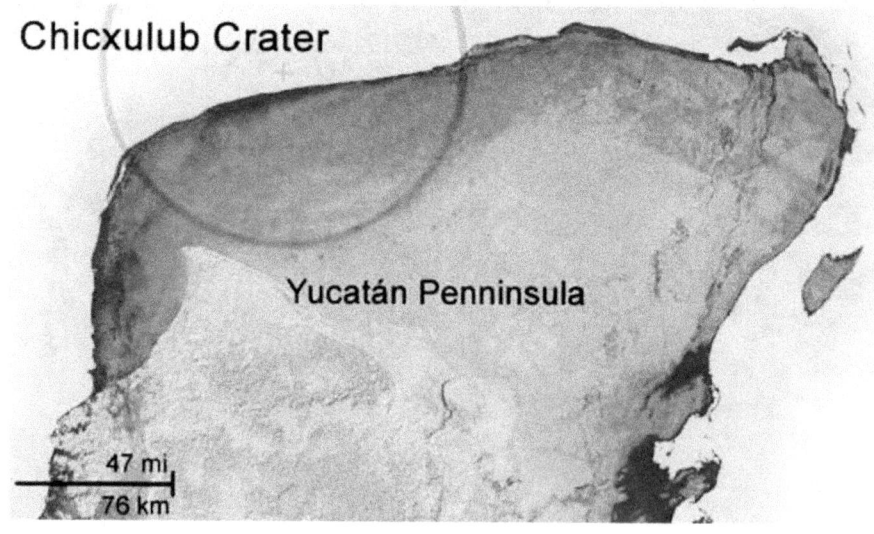

Chicxulub Crater

Yucatán Penninsula

47 mi
76 km

Some of the findings and analysis may be summarized as follows.

Atmosphere

Studies of the impact conclude that dense clouds of dust blocked the sun's rays, darkening and chilling Earth to deadly levels for most plants and, in turn, many animals. Then, when the dust finally settled, greenhouse gases created by the impact caused temperatures to skyrocket above pre-impact levels.

In just a few years, according to this hypothesis, these frigid and sweltering climatic extremes caused the extinction of up to 70 percent of all plants and animals living at the time.

Iridium

One of the key factors in proving the asteroid impact is the layer of iridium found deposited at the same time of the impact.

This evidence for the impact was first discovered by Walter Alvarez and colleagues. They found that rocks laid down precisely at the K-T boundary contain extraordinary amounts of the metal iridium all over the world, including boundary rocks on land and under the sea.

The dating is precise, and the iridium layer has been identified in more than 100 places around the Earth. Where the boundary is in marine sediments, the iridium occurs in a layer just above the last Cretaceous microfossils, and the sediments above it contain Paleocene microfossils from the earliest part of the Cenozoic.

The iridium is present only in the boundary rocks and therefore was deposited in a single large spike of a very short event.

Iridium occurs in normal seafloor sediments in microscopic quantities, but the iridium spike at the K-T boundary is very large.

Iridium is rare on Earth's surface but is more common in asteroids and in molten rock deep within the planet.

Scientists have discovered levels of iridium 30 times greater than average in the layer of sedimentary rock laid down at the time of the dinosaur extinction.

Melted Rock

Pieces of once-molten rock, called impact ejecta, are evidence of an explosion powerful enough to instantly melt bedrock and propel it more than a hundred miles from its origin.

Ranging in size from large chunks to tiny beads, impact ejecta are common at or near the geological layer that defines the dinosaur extinction.

Fractured Crystals

Fractured crystals, often called "shocked quartz," found at the impact site show a distinctive pattern of fracturing caused by high-energy impacts or explosions.

Some scientists maintain that the fracture pattern in these quartz crystals could only have been caused by a massive asteroid or comet impact. The pattern is prevalent in quartz found at or near the geological layer deposited at the time of the extinction.

Fossil Record

A gradual decline in the number of dinosaur species would likely mirror an equally gradual cause of their ultimate extinction. Conversely, a sudden "now you see them, now you don't" end to the dinosaurs implies a catastrophic cause.

Some paleontologists see evidence in the fossil record that dinosaurs were doing quite well prior to the end of the impact and that they were in no way declining in abundance when the impact occurred.

Astronomical Origin of Asteroid

It has been suggested by Bottke, Vokrouhlicky and Nesvorny that a collision in the asteroid belt 160 million years ago resulted in the Baptistina Family of asteroids. The largest member of this group of asteroids is 298 Baptistina.

They proposed that the "Chicxulub asteroid" which killed the dinosaurs was also a member of this group. The connection between Chicxulub and Baptistina is supported by the large amount of carbonaceous material present in microscopic fragments of the impactor, suggesting the impactor was a member of this rare class of asteroids called carbonaceous chondrites, like Baptistina.

Not all scientists are in agreement with this origin. But it is not really important; the important fact is that there are an innumerable number of potential Earth impactors.

Conclusions

This impact that killed the dinosaurs was not all bad. It allowed mammals to move to center stage that eventually led to mankind.

And it gave us the scientific warning that such an impact will most likely destroy all of mankind just as Revelation in the Bible foretells.

Chapter 11
Multiple Simultaneous Impacts Theory

The one unchangeable certainty is that nothing is unchangeable or certain. **John F. Kennedy**

It should be noted that some believe that this Chicxulub impact just described may only be one of multiple impacts that occurred at the same time. They believe that there were at least 4 large asteroids, or comet parts that broke up and became the following:

Chicxulub in Mexico;

Silverpit Crater in the North Sea;

Boltysh Crater in the Ukraine; and

Shiva Crater which consists of two parts that lie beneath the Indian continental shelf and the Indian Ocean west of Mumbai, India.

The Chicxulub has already been described.

Silverpit Crater

Silverpit crater is a buried sub-sea structure under the North Sea off the coast of the United Kingdom. The crater-like form, named after the Silver Pit which is a nearby sea-floor valley recognized by generations of fishermen, was discovered during the routine exploration for gas in the Southern North Sea Sedimentary Basin.

Its age is between 74 and 45 million years, however, the interpretation is somewhat controversial.

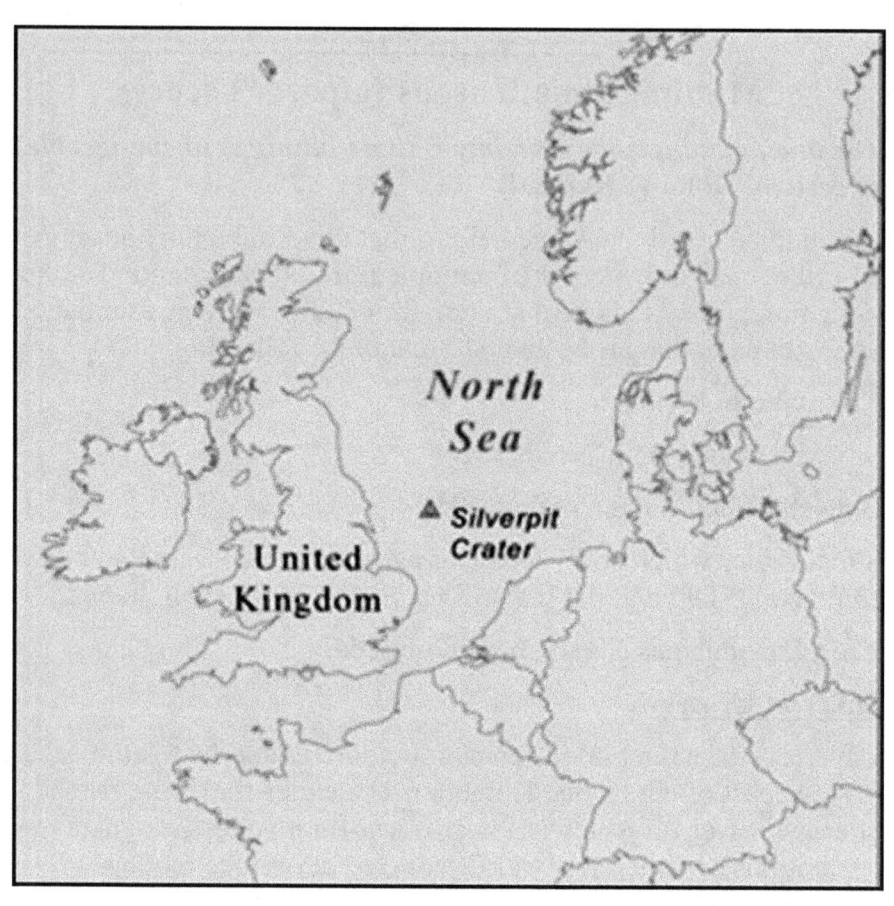

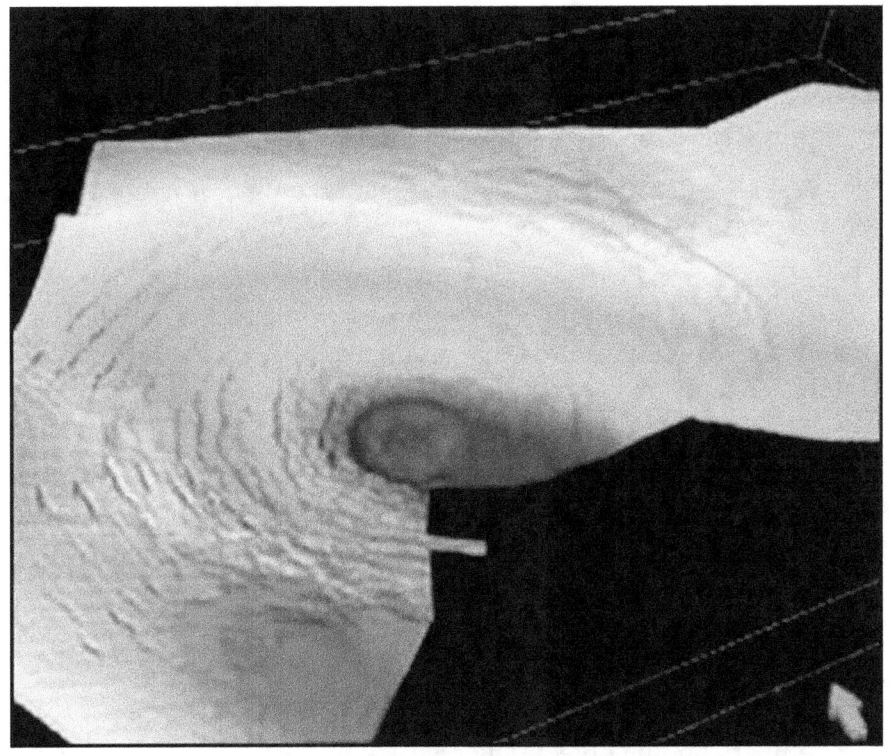

A perspective view of the top chalk surface, looking north-east, shows the central crater and its surrounding rings. Colors have been added to indicate depth with red/yellow meaning shallow and blue/purple meaning deep. (Image credit: Phil Allen (PGL) and Simon Stewart (BP))

The crater-like structure was discovered by petroleum geoscientists Simon Stewart of BP and Philip Allen, then of Production Geosciences Ltd, during routine analysis of seismic data while exploring for natural gas deposits in a region 130 kilometers off the Humber estuary.

Allen noticed an unusual set of concentric rings. Although they looked like they may have been caused by a meteor, he had no experience of impact structures. So he hung an image of them on the wall of his office, hoping someone else might be able to shed light on the mystery. Stewart, visiting Production Geosciences on an unrelated matter, had long predicted that a crater would be found on 3D seismic data, saw the image and suggested it might be an impact feature. The discovery of the crater and the impact hypothesis were reported in the journal Nature in 2002.

Stewart and Allen's studies suggest that at the time of its formation the area was under less than 50 to 300 meters of water.

The presence of a central peak, something that Stewart & Allen contend is difficult to form except through a meteorite impact provided a strong indication that an impact had created the crater. But this conclusion is continued to be debated.

If one assumes the meteor impact theory is right, the size of the crater can be combined with assumptions about the speed of an impacting object to estimate the size of the impactor itself. Impacting objects are generally moving at speeds of the order of 20 to 50 kilometers per second, and at these speeds an object about 120 meters across would be required to form a Silverpit-sized crater, if the object was rocky. If it had been a comet, the crater would have been larger.

For comparison, the object which struck the Earth at Chicxulub is estimated to have measured approximately 9.6 kilometers across, while the object responsible for the Tunguska event in Russia in 1908, and described later, is thought to have been a comet or asteroid about 60 meters across.

This impact would have generated enormous tsunamis but no such evidence has yet been found.

It should be noted that Silverpit bears a stronger resemblance to the Valhalla crater on Jupiter's moon Callisto than it does to other terrestrial craters

The early estimate of the age of the Silverpit event, stated as 65-60 million years before present, overlaps with the age of the Chicxulub impact, which occurred 65 million years ago.

Several other large impact craters of around the same age have been discovered, all between latitudes 20 N and 70 N, leading to the speculative hypothesis that the dinosaurs killing Chicxulub impact may have been only one of several impacts that happened all at the same time.

The collision of Comet Shoemaker-Levy 9 with Jupiter in 1994, as we describe later, proved that gravitational interactions can fragment a comet and give rise to several impacts over a period of a few days if the comet fragments should collide with a planet.

Let's look at some of the other possible companion impacts.

Boltysh Crater

The Boltysh Crater is an impact crater in the Kirovohrad Oblast of Ukraine. The crater is 24 kilometers in diameter and its age has been determined to be about 65.2 million years, based on argon dating techniques. It is within statistical error of that of the Chicxulub Crater in Mexico.

Boltysh Crater is located in central Ukraine, in the basin of the Tiasmyn River, a tributary of the Dnieper River. It is 24 kilometers in diameter, and is surrounded by an ejecta blanket of breccia preserved over an area of 6,500 square kilometers. It is estimated that immediately after the impact, ejecta covered an area of 25,000 square kilometers to a depth of 1 meter or greater, and was some 600 meters deep at the crater rim.

The crater contains a central uplift about 6 kilometers in diameter, rising about 550 meters above the base level of the crater. This uplift currently lies beneath about 500 meters of sediment deposited since the impact, and was discovered in the 1960s while exploring of oil shale deposits.

Shiva Crater

The Shiva crater is a geologic impact structure of about 500 kilometers in diameter. This geologic structure consists of the Bombay High and Surat Depression. They lie beneath the Indian continental shelf and the Indian Ocean west of Mumbai, India and east of Africa and the Island of Madagascar. The structure was named after Shiva, the Hindu god of destruction and renewal.

Area of Shiva Crater Shown on Google Earth

It is believed that this Shiva crater was created around 65 million years ago, about the same time as a number of other impact craters that caused the Cretaceous-Paleocene extinction event that killed the dinosaurs.

Although the site has shifted since its formation because of sea floor spreading, the formation is approximately 600 kilometers long by 400 kilometers wide. It is estimated that this crater would have been made by an asteroid or comet approximately 40 kilometers in diameter.

Some Earth scientists question whether Shiva Crater is indeed an impact crater.

Unlike typical known extraterrestrial impact structures, Shiva is teardrop shaped, roughly 600 kilometers by 400 kilometers. Some believe that this was caused by the low angle of the impact combined with boundary fault lines and unstable rock.

Other researchers have also noted that rock faults and impacts could modify the crater shape. The crater also is reported to contain larger than average amounts of alkaline melt rocks, shocked quartz, and iron oxide laced with iridium. These types of rocks and features suggest an impact origin.

The age of the crater is inferred from the Deccan traps, which contain relatively high amounts of iridium which is extremely rare in the Earth's crust but more common in asteroids.

Conclusion

The Shiva Crater and the other possible impact craters along with the Chicxulub have led to the hypothesis that multiple impacts caused the massive extinction event at the end of the Cretaceous period including extinction of the dinosaurs.

It should also be noted that Shiva's impact was enough to cause the mass extinction all by itself.

This has led to the suggestion that the Chicxulub impact was one of several that occurred almost simultaneously, perhaps due to a disrupted comet impacting the Earth in a similar manner to the collision of Comet Shoemaker-Levy 9 with Jupiter in 1994.

We will discuss Comet Shoemaker-Levy more later.

Chapter 12
Arizona Asteroid of 50 Thousand Years Ago

The third angel sounded his trumpet, and a great star, blazing like a torch, fell from the sky... **Revelation 8:10**

This Meteor Crater in Arizona has been named Barringer Crater in honor of Daniel Barringer, who was first to suggest in 1906 that it was produced by a meteorite impact.

However it was not until 1960 that later research by Eugene Merle Shoemaker confirmed Barringer's hypothesis that the crater was from the impact of a meteorite.

The key confirming factor was the discovery in the crater of the minerals coesite and stishovite which are rare forms of silica found only where quartz-bearing rocks have been severely shocked by an instantaneous overpressure. It cannot be created by volcanic action; the only known natural mechanism of creating it is through an impact event.

Shoemaker's discovery is considered the first definitive proof of an extraterrestrial impact on the Earth's surface. Since then, numerous impact craters have been identified around the world, though Meteor Crater remains one of the most visually impressive because of its size, young age, and lack of vegetative cover.

The crater is 1.186 kilometers in diameter and was created about 50 thousand years ago.

The largest fragment discovered from the meteorite that formed Meteor Crater has been named the Holsinger meteorite and is exhibited at the Meteor Crater tourist center in Flagstaff, Arizona.

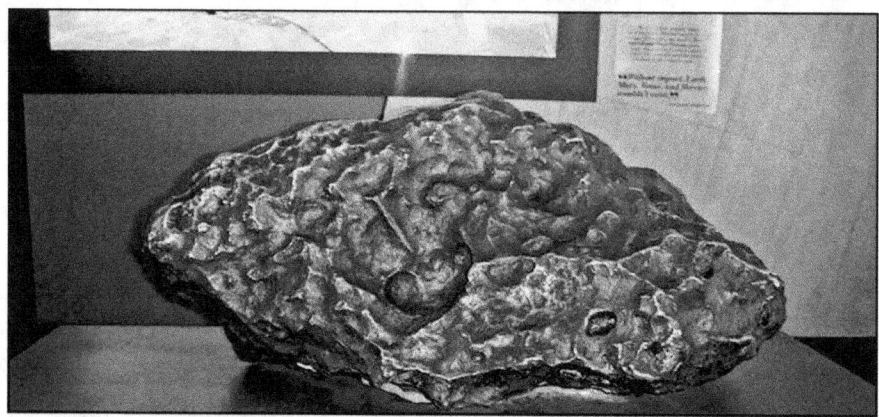

The Barringer Meteor Crater is approximately 43 miles east of Flagstaff, Arizona.

Meteor Crater lies at an elevation of about 1,740 meters above sea level. It is about 1,200 meters in diameter and about 170 meters deep and is surrounded by a rim that rises 45 meters above the surrounding plains. The center of the crater is filled with 210 to 240 meters of rubble lying above the crater bedrock.

One of the interesting features of the crater is its squared-off outline which is believed to be caused by pre-existing regional cracks in the strata at the impact site.

The meteorite that caused the crater was of nickel-iron about 50 meters in diameter. It struck the plain at a speed of several kilometers per second. Impact energy has been estimated at about 10 megatons. The speed of the impact has been a subject of some debate. Recent research suggests the impact was about 12.8

kilometers per second. It is believed that about half of the meteorite's bulk was vaporized during its descent before it hit the ground.

The remaining parts of the meteorite were mostly vaporized upon impact with very little remaining in the crater.

Chapter 13
More Recent Impacts

Civilization exists by geological consent, subject to change without notice. **Will Durant**

I have given you some feel for asteroid impacts on Earth. I believe, however that we need to look at some more recent impacts to show that asteroid impacts are not just a thing of the past.

I therefore describe 5 additional impacts that have been more recent.

1. Henbury in Australia 7,600 years ago;

2. Rio Cuarto Crater Group in Argentina 10,000 years ago;

3. Kaali Crater Group in Argentina 4,000 to 7,600 years ago;

4. Russian Tunguska Asteroid of 1908; and

5. The Chelyabinsk Asteroid of 2013.

Henbury Meteorites Conservation Reserve

Henbury Meteorites Conservation Reserve is a protected area in the Northern Territory of Australia. The reserve is located 145 kilometers south west of Alice Springs and contains twelve craters, which were formed when a fragmented meteorite hit the Earth's surface.

Henbury is one of five meteorite impact sites in Australia associated with actual meteorite fragments and one of the world's best preserved examples of a small crater field.

At Henbury there are 13 to 14 craters ranging from 7 to 180 meters in diameter and up to 15 meters in depth that were formed when the meteor broke up before impact.

Several tons of iron-nickel fragments have been recovered from the site. The site has been dated to about 4200 years ago based on the cosmogenic 14 Carbon terrestrial age of the meteorite.

The craters are named for Henbury Station, a nearby cattle station named in 1875 for the family home of its founders in England.

This is the largest crater at the impact site.

Here's another view.

Rio Cuarto Craters

The Río Cuarto Craters are a group of impact craters located in Córdoba Province, Argentina.

There are ten depressions of which four are of substantial size. One crater, named the "Drop", is about 200 meters wide and 600 meters long. Two more large craters, the "Eastern Twin" and "Western Twin", both about 700 meters wide and 3.5 kilometers long, were located 5 kilometers to the northeast.

Another major crater, the "Northern Basin", about half again as big as one of the Twins, was sited 11 kilometers further to the northeast. The long axes of the craters all pointed to the northeast.

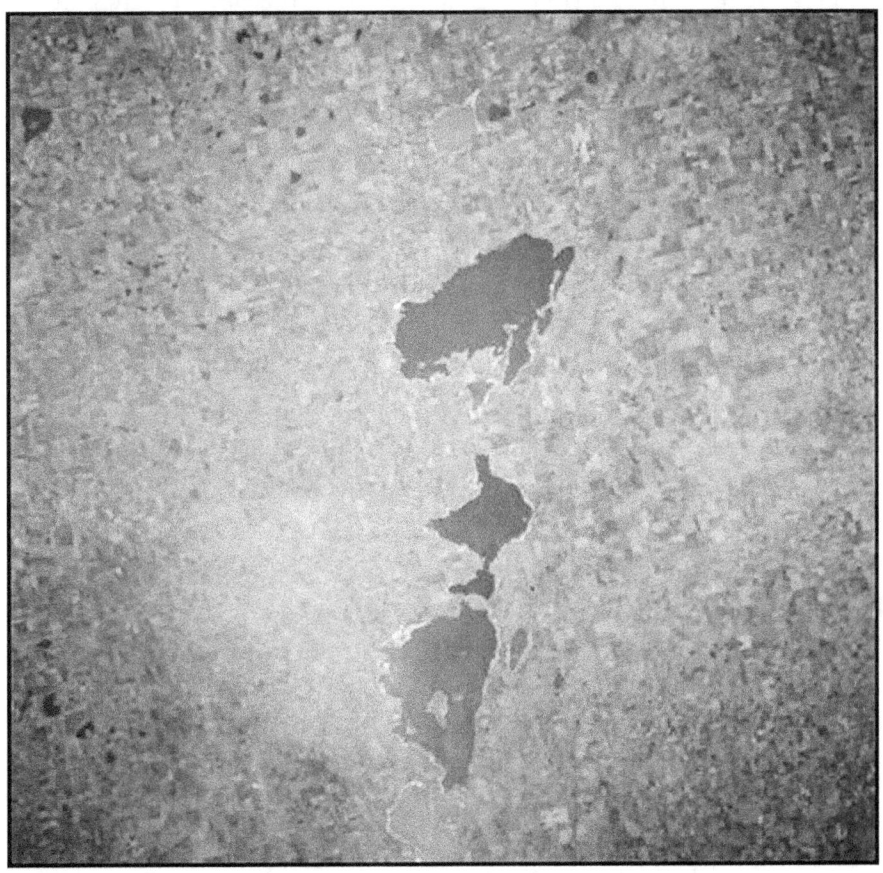

The craters are thought to be due to a grazing impact of a set of objects at a very low angle, which calculations show to be a rare occurrence. Most impacts will strike at an angle of 45 degrees to the horizontal or greater, and the impact craters will always be close to circular, since the shock wave that results from the impact propagates symmetrically.

This northeast-southwest aligned string of lakes spanning about 30 kilometers is the result of these meteorite craters. The lakes range in size from a few kilometers to about 250 meters along their long axis. Small meteorites were found in a crater confirming the lakes impact origin.

Models of the Río Cuarto event suggest that the object struck at an angle of no more than 15 degrees from the horizontal, with the impact itself having 10 times more explosive energy than the Barringer Crater event and 30 times more than the Tunguska event.

Although the age of the craters has not yet been determined precisely, it is believed they are no more than 10,000 years old.

The object came in from the northeast, as bright as the Sun. The object hit ground at the Northern Basin, creating a mountain of fire about 10 kilometers wide and 50 kilometers long, and scattered off pieces that went downrange to form the Twins and the Drop.

The fireball most likely incinerated all life downrange in a firestorm with a parabolic-shaped footprint that created hurricane-force winds, erasing the butterfly-shaped pattern of debris characteristic of such low-angle strikes.

The object was most likely a carbonaceous chondritic asteroid, largely made up of simple carbon compounds and resembling something like a big lump of soot. The impact probably released huge clouds of toxic carbon monoxide that killed off wildlife in the area, assisted by heavy concentrations of toxic nitric oxides created through ionization by the object's fiery passage through the atmosphere.

It is likely the impact resulted in serious atmospheric effects and may have even had a short-term effect on global climate.

Kaali Crater Group

Kaali is a group of 9 meteorite craters located in the village of Kaali on the Estonian island of Saaremaa. It was formed more than 4,000 years ago and possibly as long as 7,600 years ago.

The main crater is nearly circular.

When the water level is low, rocks can be seen penetrating the surface: in the middle of one of the craters.

It is a comparatively recent crater created by an impact event that is possibly the only known major impact event that has occurred in a populated area.

The meteorite arrived from the north-east at an altitude of 5 to 10 kilometers. It broke into pieces and fell to the Earth in fragments, the greatest of which produced a crater with a diameter of 110 meters and a depth of 22 meters.

The explosion removed approximately 81 000 cubic meters of dolomite and other rocks and formed 7 to 8 kilometers tall, extremely hot gas flow. Vegetation was incinerated up to 6 kilometers from the impact site.

Kaali Lake exists at the bottom of this crater.

Eight smaller craters are also associated with this bombardment. Their diameters range from 12 to 40 meters and their respective depths vary from one to four meters. They are all within one kilometer of the main crater.

Its impact energy is comparable with that of the Hiroshima bomb blast.

Scholars maintain that the event figured prominently in regional mythology. It was, and still is, considered a sacred lake. There is archaeological evidence that it may well have been a place of ritual sacrifice.

At some point during the early Iron Age, the lake was surrounded by a stone wall measuring 470 meters in length, with a median width of about 2.5 meters and an average height of 2.0 meters.

Finnish mythology has stories that may originate with the formation of Kaali. One of them is in runes 47, 48 and 49 of the Kalevala epic which tells how Louhi, the evil wizard, steals the Sun and fire from people, causing total darkness. Ukko, the god of the sky, orders a new Sun to be made from a spark.

The virgin of the air starts to make a new Sun, but the spark drops from the sky and hits the ground. This spark goes to an "Aluen" or "Kalevan" lake and causes its water to rise.

Finnish heroes see the ball of fire falling somewhere "behind the Neva river" which is the direction of Estonia from Karelia. The heroes head that direction to seek fire, and they finally gather flames from a forest fire.

This is an interesting story that reminds us of the stories associated with those previously described.

According to a theory first proposed by Lennart Meri, it is possible that Saaremaa was the legendary Thule Island, first mentioned by ancient Greek geographer Pytheas, whereas the name "Thule" could have been connected to the Finnic word tule which means of fire. This folklore of Estonia describes ancient beliefs of the birth of the Crater Lake in Kaali. Kaali was considered the place where "The sun went to rest."

Russian Tunguska Asteroid of 1908

One of the best-known recorded impacts in modern times was the Tunguska event, which occurred in Siberia, Russia, in June of 1908. This incident involved an explosion that was probably caused by the airburst of an asteroid or comet 5 to 10 kilometers above the Earth's surface. It knocked down an estimated 80 million trees over an area of 2,150 square kilometers.

These photos of trees knocked over by the Tunguska blast is from the Soviet Academy of Science taken in 1927. (Expedition led by Leonid Kulik)

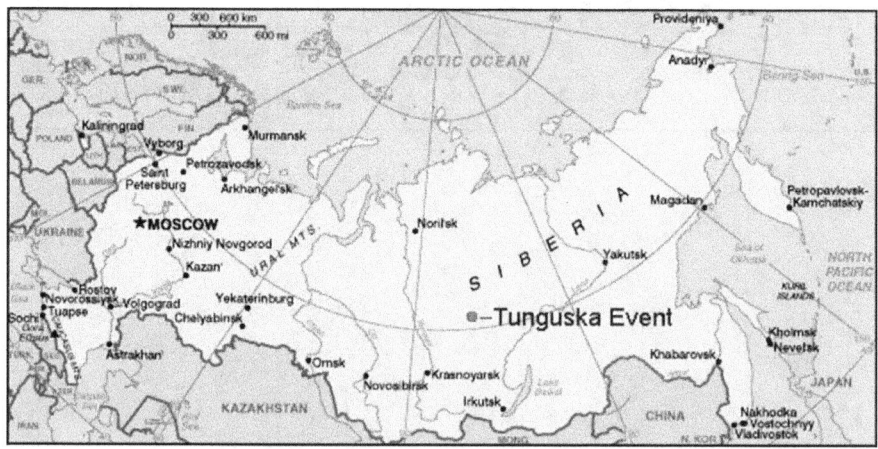

Although the meteoroid or comet appears to have burst in the air rather than hitting the surface, this event still is referred to as an impact. Estimates of the energy of the blast range from 3 to as high as 30 megatons of TNT. This would therefore have been about 1,000 times more powerful than the atomic bomb dropped on Hiroshima, Japan.

Local natives and Russian settlers in the hills northwest of Lake Baikal observed a column of bluish light, nearly as bright as the Sun, moving across the sky. About 10 minutes later there was a flash and a sound similar to artillery fire. Eyewitnesses closer to the explosion reported the sound source moving east to north. The sounds were accompanied by a shock wave that knocked people off their feet and broke windows hundreds of kilometers away.

In the United States, the Smithsonian Astrophysical Observatory and the Mount Wilson Observatory observed a decrease in atmospheric transparency that lasted for several months, from suspended dust.

In 1930, the British astronomer F.J.W. Whipple suggested that the Tunguska body was a small comet. A cometary meteorite, being composed primarily of ice and dust could have been completely vaporized by the impact with the Earth's atmosphere, leaving no obvious traces.

The comet hypothesis was further supported by the glowing skies observed across Europe for several evenings after the impact, possibly explained by dust and ice that had been dispersed from the comet's tail across the upper atmosphere.

In 1978, astronomer Ľubor Kresák suggested that the body was a fragment of the short-period Comet Encke, which is responsible for the Beta Taurid meteor shower; the Tunguska event coincided with a peak in that shower, and the approximate trajectory of the Tunguska impactor is consistent with what would be expected from such a fragment.

It is now known that bodies of this kind explode at frequent intervals tens to hundreds of kilometers above the ground. Military satellites have been observing these explosions for decades.

In 1983, astronomer Zdeněk Sekanina published a paper criticizing the comet hypothesis. He pointed out that a body composed of cometary material, travelling through the atmosphere along such a shallow trajectory, ought to have disintegrated, whereas the Tunguska body apparently remained intact into the lower atmosphere. Sekanina argued that the evidence pointed to a dense, rocky object, probably of asteroid origin.

Proponents of the comet hypothesis have suggested that the object was an extinct comet with a stony mantle that allowed it to penetrate the atmosphere.

Three-dimensional numerical modeling of the Tunguska impact done by Utyuzhnikov and Rudenko in 2008 supports the comet hypothesis. According to their results, the comet matter dispersed in the atmosphere, while the destruction of the forest was caused by the shock wave.

Chelyabinsk Russian Air Burst in 2013

A much smaller air burst occurred over a populated area in Russia on February 15, 2013, at Chelyabinsk in the Ural district of Russia. It inflicted more than 1,200 injuries, mainly from broken glass caused by the meteor's shock wave. It is estimated that it caused over $33 million in damages.

**Trail left by the exploding Chelyabinsk Meteor
As it passed over the city**

The object's air burst occurred at an altitude between 30 and 50 kilometers above the ground. Its estimated speed was about 40,000 miles per hour. The dazzling light of the meteor was bright enough to cast moving shadows during the morning daylight in the city of Chelyabinsk. Eyewitnesses also felt intense heat from the fireball.

Its estimated energy was 20-30 times greater than was released from the atomic bombs detonated at Hiroshima and Nagasaki.

A small piece of the impactor was found by Ural Federal University scientists at Lake Chebarkul.

A 112.2 g Fragment of the Chelyabinsk Meteorite

This specimen was found on a field between the villages of Deputatsky and Emanzhelinsk on 18 February 2013. The broken fragment displays thick primary fusion crust with flow lines and a heavily shocked matrix with melt veins and planar fractures.

An additional 53 small pieces have been found in the impact area.

Dmitry Medvedev, the Prime Minister of Russia, said that this event proves the "entire planet" is vulnerable to meteors and a "Space-Guard" system is needed to protect the planet from similar objects in the future.

On the day of the impact, Bloomberg News reported that the United Nations Office for Outer Space Affairs had suggested the investigation of creating an "Action Team on Near-Earth Objects", a proposed global asteroid warning network system.

New York City planetarium director Neil deGrasse Tyson said the meteor was unpredicted because no attempt had been made to find and catalogue every 15 meter near-Earth object.

Chapter 14
Other Notable Impacts

We live in a society exquisitely dependent on science and technology, in which hardly anyone knows anything about science and technology. **Carl Sagan**

There have been many notable impacts on planet Earth. The more we can learn about them the better we can develop programs to protect against them.

I will describe 6 more to provide further insight into the dangers we face, and to give credence to what is foretold by Revelation. Then I will discuss how we may delay the inevitable.

The first 4 of the 6 additional that I will describe are:

1. The Shoemaker Crater in West Australia 568 to 1,630 Million Years Old
2. The Loner Lake in India 579 Million Years Old
3. Upheaval Dome in Utah 170 Million Years Old
4. Chesapeake Bay and Toms Canyon

Shoemaker Crater in West Australia 568 to 1,630 Million Years Ago

The Shoemaker impact structure lies in the arid, central part of Western Australia about 100 kilometers north-northeast of Wiluna, in a drainage basin south of the Waldburg Range. Below is an astronaut photograph from the NASA Earth Observatory of the structure.

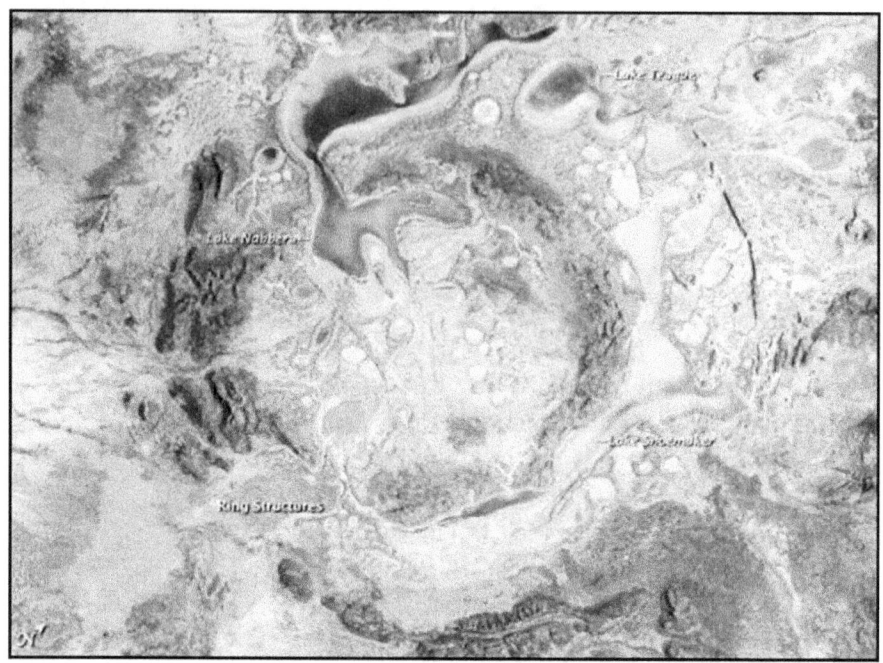

The Shoemaker impact site is approximately 30 kilometers in diameter and clearly defined by concentric ring structures formed in Precambrian sedimentary rocks (brown to dark brown, image center).

A dark, crescent-shaped inner ring surrounds the core, which consists of uplifted granitic rocks. Several saline and ephemeral lakes, Nabberu, Teague, Shoemaker, and numerous smaller ponds occupy the land surface between the ring structures. Differences in color result from both water depth and from suspended sediments, with some bright salt crusts visible around the edges of smaller ponds (image center).

The structure, formerly known as Teague Ring was renamed Shoemaker in honor of Dr. Eugene M. Shoemaker (1928-1997), a pioneer in impact crater studies and planetary geology, as well as the founder of the Astrogeology Branch of the U.S. Geological Survey.

The first suggestion that the ring-like topographic feature may be an impact structure was published in 1974. Subsequent research revealed definitive evidence for this hypothesis, including the presence of shatter cones and shocked quartz.

The age of the impact event is uncertain. It must be younger than the Teague Granite in the centre, dated at 2,648 ± 8 million years ago. The most commonly cited age of about 1,630 million years ago represents a re-heating event affecting the granite.

More recent dating by K-Ar methods yield ages as young as 568 ± 20 million years ago, however this age could date the impact event or subsequent tectonic activity.

Loner Lake in India 570 Thousand Years Old

Lonar Lake is a saline soda lake located at Lonar in Buldana district of Maharashtra, India, which was created by a meteor impact of about 570,000 years ago.

It has a mean diameter of 1.2 kilometers and is about 137 meters below the crater rim. The meteor crater rim is about 1.8 kilometers in diameter.

The circular depression bears a saline water lake in its central portion.

A series of low hills surround the basin which has an oval shape (almost round) with circumference at top of about 8 kilometers. The sides of the basin rise abruptly at an angle of about 75 degrees. At the base, the lake has a circumference of about 4.8 kilometers.

The slopes are covered with jungle that is interspersed with teak trees.

A belt of large trees about a mile broad runs all round the basin; this belt is formed of concentric rings of different species of trees: a ring of date-palms followed by a ring of tamarind trees nearly 1.6 kilometers broad. This then leads to a ring of babul gum trees bounded on the inside by a belt of bare muddy space.

This muddy space is several hundred meters broad and is devoid of all vegetation due to the soda content of the water; it is covered with a whitish slimy soil. During the rainy season, the drainage into the lake covers this muddy space.

The water of the lake contains various salts or sodas, and during dry weather when evaporation reduces the water level, large quantities of soda are collected. Two small streams drain into the lake, and a well of sweet water is located on the southern side, close to the water's edge.

Lonar Lake lies within the only known extraterrestrial impact crater found within the great Deccan Traps basaltic formation of India. The crater has an oval shape. The meteorite came from the east in a tilt of 35-40 degrees.

The lake was first mentioned in ancient scriptures such as the Skanda Purana, the Padma Puran and the Aaina-i-Akbari. The first European to visit the lake was British officer, J.E. Alexander in 1823.

The historical document called the Ain-i-Akbari, written about 1600, states:

"These Mountains produce all the requisites for making glass and soap. And here is saltpeter works which yield considerable revenue to the State, from the duties collected. On these mountains is a spring of salt water, but the water from the centre and the edges is perfectly fresh."

Numerous temples surround the lake, most of which stand in ruins today, except for the temple of Daitya Sudan at the centre of the Lonar town, which was built in honour of Vishnu's victory over the giant Lonasur.

Among the frequent visitors are the religious visitors from nearby towns and villages who are not adequately educated by the means of signboards and attending officials about littering and maintaining the beauty of this nationally important destination.

The Crater is protected as a geological landmark and authorities have recognized the role of the historical and archaeological heritage in the lake, nevertheless action is needed to prevent the adverse impact of settlements and religious festivities on local ecosystem. Various civic activities (e.g. "Save Lonar") in protection of Lonar crater are on-going.

Upheavel Dome in Utah 170 Million Years Old

Upheaval Dome is the deeply eroded remnants of an impact crater, in Canyonlands National Park southwest of the city of Moab, Utah, in the United States. The crater is approximately 42 miles by vehicle from Moab.

It is approximately 5 kilometers in diameter and is estimated to be somewhat less than 170 million years old. The crater is clearly visible on the surface as bright brown and black concentric rings.

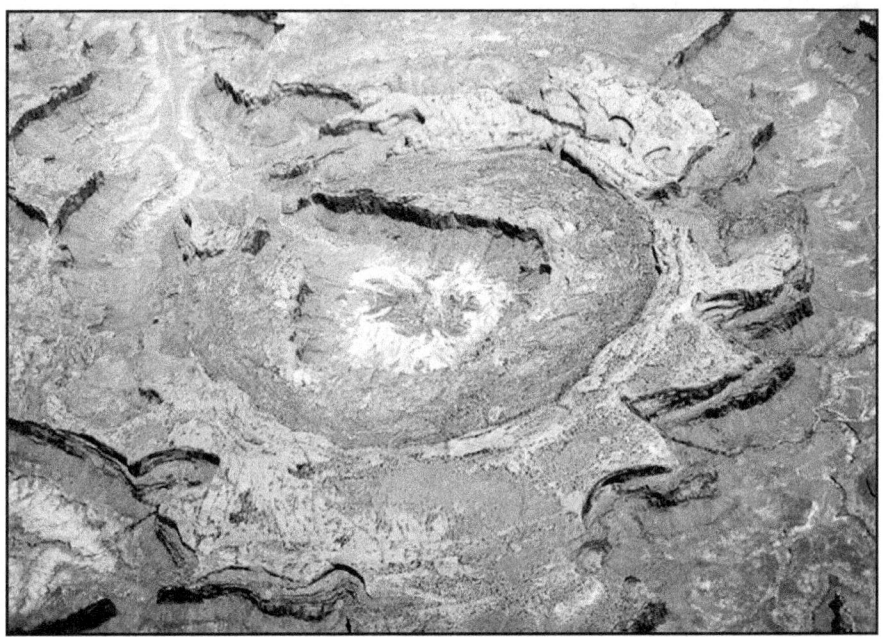

The dome is quite anomalous. Most of the rock strata of Canyonlands National Park are flat-lying or gently dipping. The center of the structure is a true dome. Some strata near the center are nearly vertical in orientation. Dips of 70 degrees have been measured in the Kayenta Formation on the U-shaped plateau surrounding the center of the structure.

A syncline or fold surrounds the center, where the axis forms a complete circle approximately two miles across. The syncline is primarily visible in the Navajo Sandstone.

Chesapeake Bay and Toms Canyon

The Chesapeake Bay impact crater as formed by an impact on the eastern shore of North America about 35 million years ago. It is one of the best-preserved "wet-target" or marine impact craters, and the largest known in the United States. Continued slumping of sediments over the rubble of the crater has helped shape the Chesapeake Bay.

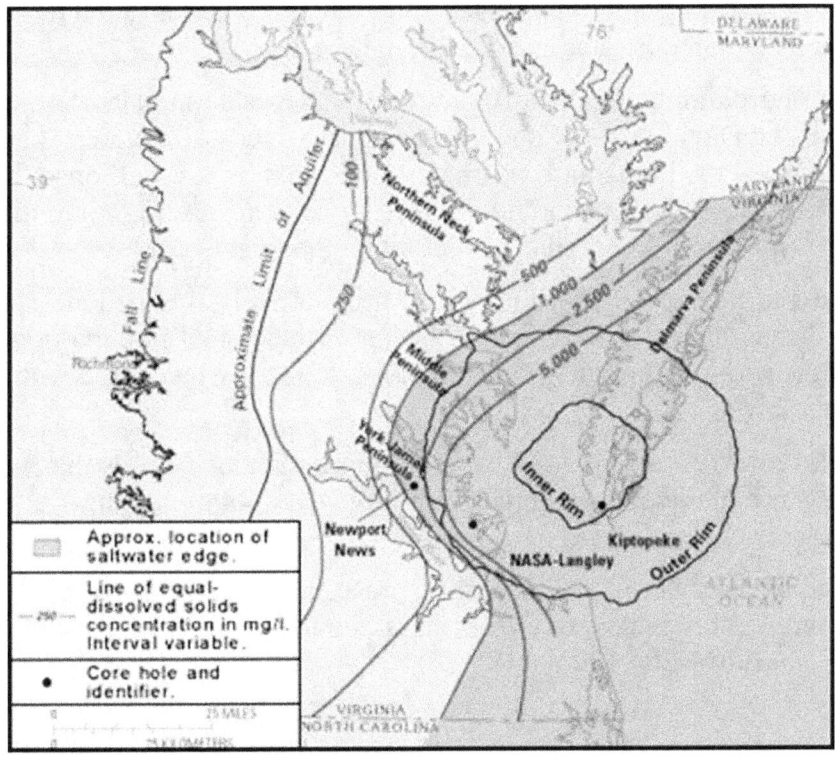

During the warm, late Eocene when the impact occurred, sea levels were high, and the Tidewater region of Virginia lay in the coastal shallows. The shore of eastern North America, about where Richmond, Virginia, is today, was covered with dense tropical rainforest, and the waters of the gently sloping continental shelf were rich with marine life that was depositing dense layers of lime from their microscopic shells.

The impact was at a speed of many kilometers per second, punching a deep hole through the sediments and into the granite continental base rock. The impactor was completely vaporized, with the base rock being fractured to depths of 8 kilometers and a peak ring was raised around it.

The deep crater, which is 38 kilometers across, is surrounded by a flat-floored terrace-like ring trough with an outer edge of collapsed blocks forming ring faults. The entire circular crater is about 85 kilometers in diameter and 1.3 kilometers deep.

The surrounding region suffered massive devastation. USGS scientist David Powers, one of the impact crater's discoverers, has described the immediate aftermath: "Within minutes, millions of tons of water, sediment, and shattered rock were cast high into the atmosphere for hundreds of miles along the East Coast."

The sedimentary walls of the crater progressively slumped in, widened the crater, and formed a layer of huge blocks on the floor of the ring-like trough. The slump blocks were then covered with the rubble.

The crater was then buried by additional sedimentary beds that have accumulated during the 35 million years following the impact.

Another, smaller impact site, the Toms Canyon impact crater, lies about 322 kilometers to the northeast, on the continental shelf off the coast of New Jersey.

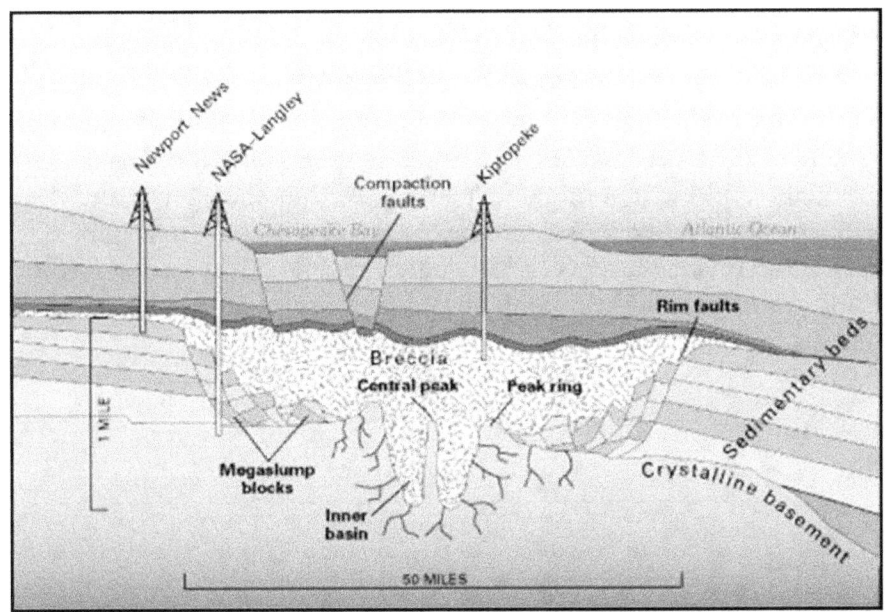

It is believed that this crater, having been dated to the late Eocene also, was formed in the same impact event as the Chesapeake Bay crater.

Until 1983, no one suspected the existence of a large impact crater buried beneath the lower part of the Chesapeake Bay and its surrounding peninsulas. The first hint was an 8 inch thick layer of ejecta that turned up in a drilling core taken off Atlantic City, New Jersey, far to the north. The layer contained the fused glass beads called tektites and shocked quartz grains that are unmistakable signs of an impact.

In 1993, data from oil exploration revealed the extent of the crater.

The continual slumping of the rubble within the crater has affected the flow of the rivers and shaped the Chesapeake Bay. The impact crater created a long-lasting topographic depression which helped predetermine the course of local rivers and the eventual location of Chesapeake Bay. Most important for present-day inhabitants of the area, the impact disrupted aquifers. The present freshwater aquifers lie above deep, salty brine, making the entire lower Chesapeake Bay area susceptible to groundwater contamination.

The crater is also one of three factors contributing to the sinking of land near the Chesapeake Bay. For example, Hampton Roads is gradually sinking at a rate between 5 and 7.5 inches per century. This is occurring because of the slippage of the coast into the crater, the reverse effects of "isostatic rebound" of the crust of the Earth from the weight of long absent glaciers north of Maryland, and groundwater removal.

Chapter 15
Earth's Largest Impact Fields

Asteroids are the vermin of the skies. **Walter Baade**

So we know that Earth has been impacted by asteroids and other bodies from heaven many, many times.

Perhaps I have shown enough, but I would like to end the impact discussion by describing Earth's largest impact fields.

The Pultusk impact field has the largest number of impacts ever found in one place. However, the Australasian is the largest impact field from an area standpoint.

Pultusk, Largest Number of Impacts in One Place

The Pultusk Meteorite fell January 30, 1868 near the town of Pultusk which is about 60 kilometers northeast of Warsaw, Poland. Thousands of people witnessed the large fireball followed by detonations and a very large shower of small fragments falling on ice, land and houses within an area of about 127 square kilometers. The estimated number of fragments was 68,780.

The fragments ranged in weight from half a gram to over 9 kilograms, about 20 pounds.

The overall estimated mass of the meteorites was 8,863 kilograms (19,540 pounds).

The Pultusk meteorite is the largest stony meteorite shower ever recorded.

Pultusk Meteorite Samples on Display

Australasian Largest Impact Field

The Australasian meteorite field covers at least one-tenth of the Earth's surface. It is the largest, and the youngest, ever found. This 800,000 year-old field includes most of Southeast Asia (Vietnam, Thailand, Southern China, Laos and Cambodia).

The material from the impact stretches across the ocean to include the islands of the Philippines, Indonesia, Malaysia and Java and reaches far out into the Indian Ocean and south to the western side of Australia.

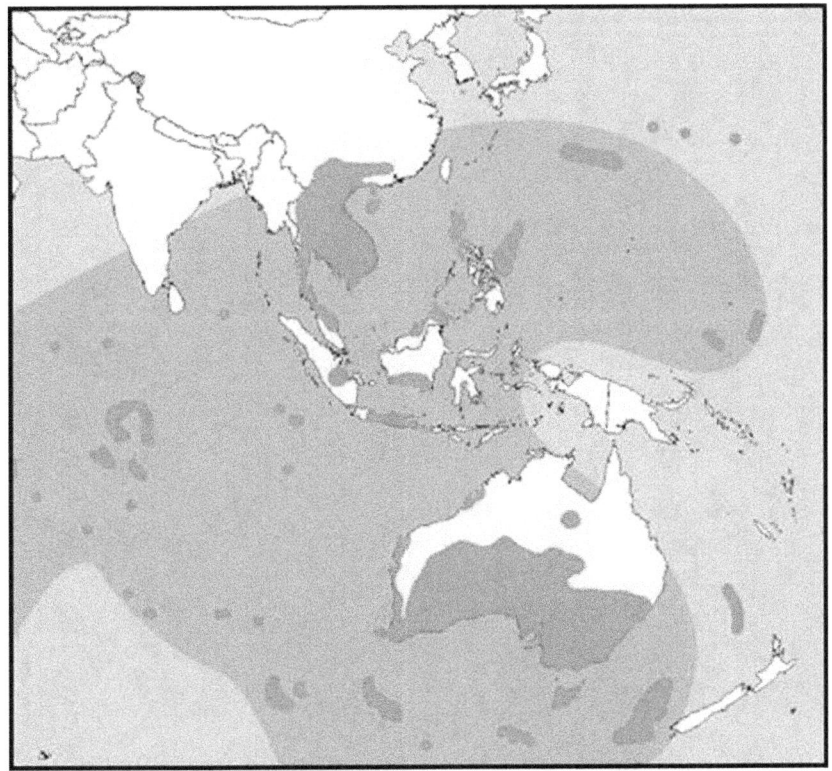

Australasian Impact (Strewn Field)

The impact crater may have been between 32 and 114 kilometers in diameter. Also, some recent estimates suggest that the strewn field may cover 30% of the Earth's surface.

Chapter 16
Conclusions About Revelation Forecast

"Philosophers and theologians have yet to learn that a physical fact is as sacred as a moral principle." **J. Louis Agassiz**

Will the forecast of Revelation become true? Will we be destroyed by an asteroid?

Yes, absolutely. Based on the history of asteroid impacts on planet Earth we can reach no other conclusion.

John found ancient documents and wrote about the asteroid that had the greatest impact on humans. He predicted that it would happen again.

Many ancient documents describe that great destruction.

The history of asteroid impacts on Earth proves that such impacts happen again and again. They come in all sizes. A giant destroyed the dinosaurs 65 million years ago. A smaller one hit in Russia and caused damage in 2013.

Many, many have impacted Earth between these times.

The statistics tell us that we will be destroyed by an asteroid impact. It is just a matter of time.

A survey April 21-26, 2010 found that 31% of Americans believed that an asteroid will collide with Earth by 2050. A 61% majority disagreed.

Not everyone understands statistics or history.

Chapter 17
Can We Counter Revelation and Save Earth

The dinosaurs became extinct because they didn't have a space program. And if we become extinct because we don't have a space program, it'll serve us right! **Larry Niven**

In 2000 NASA announced new data about large asteroids. "We now believe there are between 500 and 1,000 near-Earth asteroids larger than one kilometer in diameter."

Only about 40 percent of the kilometer-plus objects are known; most of the rest are expected to be identified within 10 years. At present, no known planet-killing asteroids in this size range, or any size, for that matter, is on a collision path with Earth.

Optimists say that impacts that would cause a global catastrophe (defined as killing more than one-quarter of humanity); will occur about every 330,000 years.

We will probably be able to detect such large asteroids as they approach. But our inability to detect smaller ones like the one that hit Siberia in 1908, and did great damage, will likely continue far into the future.

So What Can We Do

Perhaps the best idea for defending Earth from asteroids on a collision path with Earth is to try to deflect them with nuclear bombs.

The idea is not to disintegrate the asteroid, but rather to cook one side so hot that lots of material would vaporize and shoot off into space. In accord with the laws of mechanics, that motion would cause an equal and opposite motion that could alter the asteroid's trajectory enough to miss Earth.

Depending on the accuracy of the orbital predictions and explosion, it might be best to strike an asteroid many millions of miles distant, at which point a gentle nudge could have the desired effect.

Such ability will require very early trajectory predictions.

The Spacewatch program is now attempting a statistical survey of 100 meter and larger asteroids.

One scientist, Gehrels says: "The asteroid hazard is the most serious thing that humanity faces, because it's the only one that can eliminate society at once. But we are on the way to taking care of it."

Hurry!

Epilog

This planet is 15 million years overdue for an asteroid strike like the one that killed the dinosaurs. **L. Neil Smith**

Revelation in the Bible tells that an asteroid will destroy us.

The history of impacts on Earth and on extra-territorial planets, moons and other heavenly bodies tell us that it is only a matter of time before a civilization destroying asteroid will hit us.

Recent asteroid impacts such as the 1908 impact in Russia, and especially the very recent 2013 impact in Russia, has heightened our awareness of the dangers.

As awareness of the danger grows, and proper world leaders work together, we will eventually develop a joint program to counter this great threat. The program will consist of two major steps: early detection of the approach of threatening impacts, and a long range space craft to intercept the approaching object and deflect its trajectory with a nuclear weapon.

Our success will depend on how long it takes to convince world leaders to begin the developments. We may need another impact to further motivate project development.

Hopefully the next "motivating impact" will leave enough of us alive to start the project.

Success is also dependent on whether Revelation is a foretold promise or just a warning.

How strongly do you believe in asteroid statistics?

How strongly do you believe in Revelation and the Bible?

About the Author

Hi! Thanks so much for your interest in my books!

My principal interests are true stories of the unusual or of the previously Unknown or unexplained. I have occasionally also written some fiction.

I was born in Memphis Tennessee and grew up in Saltillo Mississippi, a small town near Tupelo Mississippi.

After graduating from Mississippi State University as an aerospace engineer I moved to Orlando Florida and worked for Lockheed Martin for 24 years. I advanced from an aerospace engineer to a Vice President of the Company and President of the Tactical Weapons Systems Division.

I then formed Parks-Jaggers Aerospace Company and sold it 4 years later.

I continued my education throughout my career with a MBA degree from Rollins College and with Post Graduate Studies in Astrophysics at UCLA; Laser Physics at the University of Michigan; Computer Science at the University of Florida; and Finance and Accounting at the Wharton School, University of Pennsylvania.

After selling my aerospace company I formed Quest Studios, Quest Entertainment and Rosebud Entertainment to make films at

Universal Studios. I produced 10 films, directed 7 films and wrote 5 films produced at Universal Studios.

I then formed UnknownTruths Publishing Company to publish true stories of the unusual or of the previously Unknown or unexplained. These include books about past events so unbelievable that most people have relegated them to "myths".

I have published 27 books with 25 in eBook format, 16 in Paperback format and 22 as Audio Books.

Jesus the Missing Years

Atlantis the Eyewitnesses

Atlantis the Eyewitnesses Part I: Creation

Atlantis the Eyewitnesses Part II: Legacy

Atlantis the Eyewitnesses Part III: Destruction

Immortal Again

Aging is a Treatable Disease

Paranormal Portal to a Parallel Universe

Alligator Attack!

The Devil Takes the Bodies

Caribbean Ghost, Genetic Memory Comes Alive

Clan of the Bigfoot

The Body Returns, Corpus de Licti

I Look Marvelous, Skin Care Guide

Indian Massacre in Orlando

Who the Hell is Satan

Noah's Flood, the Conclusive Evidence

Jesus, His School Years

Treasure Hunt, Finding Solomon's Temple Treasure

Ancient Secrets

The Birth of Jesus, A New Christian Holiday

Finding the Soul, Surviving Death

Hormones Working for You

Cain's Wife Lilith's Daughter

Reagan's Star Wars

Life and the Universe

My Blogs:
MyUnknowntruths.wordpress.com/
Unknowntruths.wordpress.com/
AtlantisEyeWitnesses.wordpress.com/
AgingIsATreatableDisease.blogspot.com/

My Websites:
UnknownTruths.com
AtlantisEyewitnesses.com
AncientSecretsBook.com
ParanormalPortalParallelUniverse.com

I have an additional 12 books in development including the following:

Aging is Preventable describes how our new knowledge of the human aging process and supplementation protocols can essentially stop aging.

End of Honor, Death of the Mafia is a true story about how the Mafia lost its honor when its members talked during the Rudy Giuliani trials.

Federal Rat describes the true story of the life and capers of a career criminal and how he became an informant and manipulated the Federal Justice System to keep getting out of prison and returning to his life of crime.

Eden Evolution addresses the questions: how did mankind really get started; was there a Garden of Eden?

Sex in the Ancient Churches describes how the ancients recognized that sex and the sun produced life and how they used both in their rituals and places of worship.

Ted Kennedy The Lion of Privilege is the true story of how Ted Kennedy and Jack Valenti misused the FBI and the IRS to close down a film production company to prevent them from making the film **Death at Chappaquiddick.**

Our Privileged Congress describes the privileges Congress has given itself without regard to benefits for the American People.

Crystal Healing describes the science of (potentially) healing crystals.

Shakma, Filming a Crazed Baboon describes the frustrating experience of making the film Shakma at Universal Studios with a crazed baboon.

How to Make a Zombie describes the science of how to make a true zombie and describes actual instances.

<u>Dam I Didn't Know That</u> describes interesting tidbits that most people do not know but are important enough to know.

<u>Alien Arrival, the First Visit</u> is a novel about alien encounters through the ages, and today.

About
UnKnownTruths
Publishing Company

UnKnownTruths Publishing Company was formed to publish true stories of the unusual or of the previously Unknown or unexplained. These stories typically provide radically different views from those that have shaped the understandings of our natural world, our religions, our science, our history, and even the foundations of our civilizations.

The Company's stories also include stories of the very important anti-aging, life-extending medical breakthroughs; stem cell therapies; genetic therapies; cloning and other emerging findings that promise to change the very meaning of life.

The Company also publishes stories from the past that are so unbelievable that they are generally considered to be myths. The published stories provide the evidence for the truth.

The Company has published 27 books with 25 in eBook format, 16 in Paperback format and 22 as Audio Books.

The Company currently has an additional 12 books in development.

UnknownTruths.com

www.ingramcontent.com/pod-product-compliance
Lightning Source LLC
Chambersburg PA
CBHW070640290526
45790CB00001B/154